Argue with Me

Argument as a Path to Developing Students' Thinking and Writing

. . .

Deanna Kuhn

Laura Hemberger | Valerie Khait

Library of Congress Cataloging-in-Publication Data

Kuhn, Deanna

   Argue with Me / Deanna Kuhn with Laura Hemberger and Valerie Khait

      p. cm.

   ISBN: 978-0-9882902-3-5

      1. Argue with Me. I. Title: Argument as a Path to Developing Students' Thinking and Writing. II. Deanna Kuhn / Laura Hemberger / Valerie Khait

Editor: Lyn Maize

Copy Editor: Christy Goldfinch

Book / Cover Design: Anna Botelho

Table of contents

Appendices

Preface

I N THIS BOOK WE PRESENT A CURRICULUM TO DEVELOP SKILLS of argumentation in precollege students, skills that now figure prominently in new U.S. education standards. The curriculum has now been implemented in a range of middle schools, and it has a substantial body of research evidence to document its effectiveness, a more rigorous and comprehensive body of evidence than is normally available for new curricula. We aim to present the curriculum in sufficient detail, with inclusion of a variety of supporting material for classroom use, such that teachers will have the information they need to implement the curriculum. The flexibility of the curriculum is emphasized throughout, with suggestions of how teachers can adapt it to their particular students and circumstances. With appropriate content it can be situated within ELA, social studies, or science classes or, as we have done, as a free-standing class addressed to intellectual skills. It is suitable for use from the middle grades through high school and can be used productively with students who are functioning in lower, middle, and upper ranges of academic performance. It is particularly fruitful in reaching disengaged, underachieving students.

In an introductory chapter, we lay the groundwork for the remaining chapters of the book. Why, we ask, should students develop argument skills, and what exactly do these skills consist of? (Readers whose objective is to learn about the curriculum itself may wish to proceed directly to Chapter 2.) In Chapter 2, we present the curriculum in broad overview, highlighting its unique features and the rationale underlying each of them. Our intent is to convey not simply the "what" to do, but also the "why."

In Chapter 3, we present the curriculum in "nuts and bolts" form, with enough concrete detail that teachers will feel confident in trying it out in their own classrooms. Accompanying the descriptions of each of the sequence of activities is easily accessible video material (look for video icons) that brings each segment to life, so readers can see exactly how it happens in a classroom. These videos include both teacher's instructions and students' activities. Included in the chapter are samples of students' written work. Also included in the book is an appendix containing materials for use in implementing the curriculum. Finally, we also include cross-referencing of items from the Common Core Standards and the Next Generation Science Standards that map onto the individual goals and activities that make up the curriculum.

In Chapter 4, we illustrate the progress in expository writing we have observed among middle-school students engaged in the curriculum over a two-year period. In Chapter 5, we illustrate students' parallel progress in argumentive discourse with one another, highlighting its function as a bridge to their development in individual written argument.

Chapter 6 presents a brief summary of the more formal research evidence documenting student gains. The assessment tools described are ones teachers may wish to adopt for their own use. In a final Chapter 7, we reflect more broadly on the student gains we have observed and their significance.

Finally, a word on accessing the video material. O-codes and QR codes function as links between printed text and the Internet. With O-codes, you text a simple code using a mobile phone, or enter that code into a special field at *www.ocodes.com*. With QR codes, you scan the item with a mobile phone, using any QR code scanning app. In either case, you are instantly linked to the content related to that code. Each O-code you text *from* your phone (or QR code you scan *with* your phone) is automatically saved online for future reference. O-codes are stored in a free account at *www.ocodes.com*, linked to your mobile number. You don't need to create an account before using O-codes, but if you do create a free account, you may share content by linking to Twitter, Facebook, or Evernote. QR codes are typically saved inside most QR scanning apps; some may also have sharing functionality. The O-code phone number for *Argue with Me* is **347-609-0751**. Add this number to your contact list and simply text any O-code to that number. You can test the link now by texting the O-code av1 or scanning the adjacent QR code. You will link directly to the first video excerpt. Wessex Press does not charge for using O-codes or QR codes, but your wireless carrier will apply standard text message and data rates. At the time of publication, phone access to O-codes is limited to the U.S. (and some Canadian locations). Alternatively, you may also test the link using your computer by typing av1 into the field on the *www.ocodes. com* home page. No charges apply to computer access.

Chapter 1

■ ■ ■

Why Argue?

THE NEW U.S. COMMON CORE STANDARDS, now adopted by almost all U.S. states, and along with them the Next Generation Science Standards, have left U.S. teachers both hopeful and uneasy—hopeful that the standards can deliver on their promise to improve teaching and learning but less than sure of how to make the most of them. Yet the sense is that these standards can be ignored only at one's peril. Both the mission and stakes facing teachers have intensified. To prosper in a rapidly changing world, today's teachers are told, students need to acquire not just traditional content knowledge but a wide range of so-called "21st-century skills." And teachers and schools increasingly are being held accountable for measurable results.

What's a Teacher to Do?

Teachers' uneasiness is not surprising, since the new standards stop well short of advising teachers how to achieve what the standards spell out as needing to be accomplished. The role of the standards is to define the objectives and no more, a fact stressed by the U.S. Department of Education. Yet, on the positive side, this is no small achievement. The standards in fact go well beyond content knowledge to emphasize intellectual skills of critical thinking and problem solving, with the objective of preparing students for the demanding and evolving roles that await them in 21st-century life.

What does this mean? All teachers will say they want to instill good thinking in their students. Yet good thinking as an aim of education has typically faltered once discussion gets beyond the level of generalities.[1] What, precisely, does the practice of good thinking consist of? Experts continue to debate what the 21st-century skills are that students will need.[2] But the Common Core Standards go beyond invoking global constructs like critical thinking and surpass earlier efforts to define standards by explicitly identifying core intellectual skills that students must master. A succinct example from the new standards is this one:

> *[Students should be able to]* **Write arguments to support claims with clear reasons and relevant evidence. Introduce claim(s), acknowledge alternate or opposing claims, and organize the reasons and evidence logically. Support claim(s) with logical reasoning and relevant evidence, using accurate, credible sources and demonstrating an understanding of the topic or text. [W.7.1 (a), (b), (c)]**

Now teachers have something more to work with, even if it's not clear how they should go about developing these skills in their students. Importantly, they are skills not confined to a single subject area—supporting claims with evidence is as important to language arts and history as it is to science. The thinking processes involved in coordinating claims, reasons, and evidence fall under the heading of *argument*, a term that we see, above and again below, is prominent in the new standards:

> *[Students should be able to]* **Trace and evaluate the argument and specific claims in a text, assessing whether the reasoning is sound and the evidence is relevant and sufficient to support the claims. [RI.7.8]**

Argument as an Educational Objective

Beyond seeking to meet the new standards, why should we care that children acquire skills of argument? What makes argument so important and leads the new standards to emphasize it? Consider this exchange between two young children:

> **Amy: Give me the ball. It's mine and I want it back.**
>
> **Bess: No. It's mine.**
>
> **Amy: It's not. It's mine.**
>
> **Bess: It is not.**

Whether or not we regard this exchange as a genuine argument, what's clear is that introducing physical force or an external authority are the means that are most likely to resolve it.

It's the introduction of reasons and evidence that will elevate the preceding exchange to the status of genuine argument. The use of reasons rather than force to persuade one another is a uniquely human capacity. It recognizes the role of human minds in mediating behavior. It empowers us as humans, both collectively and individually. Collectively, it enhances our ability to live together peaceably and productively. Individually, it is an essential and powerful tool that helps us to achieve our objectives. An e-mail to one's boss to persuade her that strategy A is superior to strategy B can succeed only if the arguments for and against A and B are thorough, sound, and effectively supported with evidence.

Arguing, in fact, has been claimed by cognitive scientists to be not just central to human thinking and reasoning but its central objective.[3,4] Oaksford et al.[4] characterize argument as the umbrella under which all reasoning lies; it is "the more general human process of which more specific forms of reasoning are a part." Possibly, then, the new standards are getting to the heart of the matter of thinking well. In this chapter, we only begin to address the question of why argument skills warrant a central place in the precollege curriculum. In the concluding chapter, we address this question more fully, examining the benefits of mastery of argument to students themselves, in and outside of classrooms, and to society.

What Is an Argument?

The term *argument* is used to refer to different practices and products. At one end is the term with its negative connotation: An argument is what we tell children they must avoid, by working out their differences in a constructive way. Later on, teachers introduce the term in its positive, constructive sense, the sense reflected in the above excerpts from the new Common Core Standards: An argument is a claim supported by reasons and evidence. Arguments in this sense are expected to have beneficial consequences. They hold the promise of articulating our respective beliefs, clarifying differences, and ideally even building shared understanding.

When teachers introduce the term *argument*, they can expect students to have some initial difficulty distinguishing the positive and negative uses of the term. In one study[5] we asked 6th-graders this question:

> **Two candidates, Bo and Le, are running for governor of your state. You are riding the bus with your friend. You know your friend prefers Bo. You prefer Le. Is it a good idea to discuss Bo and Le with your friend?**

Almost half of this age group responded that it was not a good idea because "You could get into an argument" or "It could ruin your friendship." Others were more favorable, seeing the situation as an opportunity to persuade your friend to your own view. Less than a third saw argument as a constructive process: "If we talk about it we might be able to come to a conclusion," in the words of one such 6th grader, the implication being that the conclusion would be a sounder one than the conclusion drawn by either person alone.

Without some discussion, then, many students will not appreciate the concept of argument in its positive sense. Teachers need to take care to lay this groundwork in introducing the language of argument. This is particularly so because there are some further distinctions to be made in defining what an argument is.

The earlier excerpt from the Common Core Standards specifies that the claim must be distinguished from alternate or opposing claims. This is a critical attribute. A claim that has no alternative is rarely worth making or defending. "Airplanes fly," for example, is such a claim, because the feature of flight capability is central to the definition of an airplane. No one needs or wants to make, or oppose, such a claim. It wouldn't even make sense to do so.

Still, this understanding is not one that we can assume young students have mastered. In one study, children were asked to choose among three options as the best explanation for how something worked.[6] For a dishwasher, for example, one choice was "They work because they make things that you put in them clean." Another was:

> **They work because the inside of the machine is really good at washing things. When you put your dishes inside and turn the dishwasher on, it makes them really clean.**

Like "Airplanes fly," these statements don't go beyond definition of the term itself. Only a third option offered more than a circular account:

> **They work because they spray hot water from lots of directions and it reaches all the dishes and silverware inside. They then get rinsed by clean water and then the machine dries them.**

Yet half the time kindergarteners chose as the best explanation one of the circular explanations, and even 4th graders did not always see the noncircular choice as superior.

Distinguishing claims that are worth arguing for from definitional statements like "Airplanes fly" and "Dishwashers wash dishes" is thus a skill that itself requires some learning. And it is a skill that will need strengthening in order to address more complex instances than the elementary ones we've just illustrated. For example, are the claims "2 + 3 = 5" or "Computers can be useful" or "Children need care" claims worth debating?

Genuine claims are ones that can reasonably be opposed. They are claims open to meaningful challenge. They go beyond definition (*Dishwashers wash dishes*) or logical truths (*2 is less than 3*) or personal taste (*Bowling is fun*). Genuine claims are those worth making and worth constructing an argument to support or to challenge.

Making and Judging Arguments

There is still more, however, to the skills of argument since we want students (and indeed all people) to be able not just to make and support their own claims with well-reasoned arguments. They also need to evaluate the claims and supporting arguments made by others. Indeed, the latter is exactly the competency that is now emphasized in the "Critical Reading" dimension of the new standards. With increased attention to nonfiction text, as well as narrative, students must be able to

> **[c]ite several pieces of textual evidence to support analysis of what the text says explic-**
>
> **itly as well as inferences drawn from the text. [RI7.1].**

Thus, both the production and comprehension dimensions of argument are well represented in the new standards, and argument figures prominently in both of the traditional English language arts subject areas of writing (production of arguments) and reading (comprehension of arguments). These same skills also figure prominently across the curriculum, in science and social studies and indeed all academic subjects. Especially in science and social studies, teachers and students face the challenge of appreciating both physical science and social science as consisting of evolving argument, rather than merely accumulated fact.

The boxed text below well illustrates the prominence of constructing and evaluating arguments in the reading and writing strands of the new standards. It is a sample question from PARCC (Partnership for Assessment of Readiness for College and Careers) Grade 7 ELA/Literacy Summative Assessment. These assessments are being developed to coordinate with the Common Core Standards and are scheduled to be ready for states to administer during the 2014–15 school year. To meet the standard required of the sample question, students must evaluate three presented arguments and produce an argument of their own. To do so students must have sufficient reading and writing competence to process and comprehend the writers' texts (which increase in complexity in corresponding items at higher grade levels) and to express their own ideas clearly enough to be understood. The new standards make clear that these expressive skills need also to be demonstrated in oral, as well as written, production.

You have read three texts describing Amelia Earhart. All three include the claim that Earhart was a brave, courageous person. The three texts are:

"Biography of Amelia Earhart"
"Earhart's Final Resting Place Believed Found"
"Amelia Earhart's Life and Disappearance"

Consider the argument each author uses to demonstrate Earhart's bravery.
    Write an essay that analyzes the strength of the arguments about Earhart's bravery in at least two of the texts. Remember to use textual evidence to support your ideas.

Developing these skills in middle school provides an essential foundation for what lies ahead in high school and beyond. Influenced by the new standards, both middle- and high-school social studies curricula are paying increasing attention to such skills, with argument at the core. In describing the skills that its Advanced Placement history examination assesses, the College Board makes explicit the foundational role of argument:

Historical thinking involves the ability to define and frame a question about the past and to address that question by constructing an argument. A plausible and persuasive argument requires a clear, comprehensive and analytical thesis, supported by relevant historical evidence—not simply evidence that supports a preferred or preconceived position. Additionally, argumentation involves the capacity to describe, analyze and evaluate the arguments of others in light of available evidence.

In the box below is a core question from the AP history examination that illustrates ways in which these skills are being assessed. Students may remember few details from their middle-school introductions to world and American history. But they need to have practiced the skills that will enable them to tackle such questions.

DIRECTIONS: Choose ONE question from this part. You are advised to spend 5 minutes planning and 30 minutes writing your answer. Cite relevant historical evidence in support of your generalizations and present your arguments clearly and logically.

1. Evaluate the impact of the Civil War on political and economic developments in TWO of the following regions:

    The South
    The North
    The West

    Focus your answer on the period between 1865 and 1900.

2. Compare and contrast US society in the 1920s and 1950s with respect to TWO of the following:

    race relations
    role of women
    consumerism

Reading, Writing, and Argument

Much has been written by and for educators on how to support development of students' expository writing. But the emphasis in the majority of these sources is on the writing itself, rather than the thinking that underlies the writing. The new standards make clear that organizing and relating claims, reasons, and evidence involve thinking, first and foremost, even though the products of this thinking need to be expressed in writing or in speech. In this book we focus squarely on the thinking underlying writing. We trace how skill in expository writing, and specifically argumentive essays, can be developed in young students with sustained engagement. Furthermore, we emphasize the link between individual argumentive writing and the dialogic argumentation that occurs between individuals. Dialog as a path to the development of argumentive writing is in fact the core idea on which our curriculum is based.

Reading a poem is easier than writing one. Ought we assume, then, that digesting others' arguments is easier than producing one's own? Might evaluating arguments even be the gateway to learning to produce them, by providing abundant examples of how others do it? A distinctive feature of this book and our method is that we in fact make the opposite claim—that producing arguments puts students on the most fruitful path to gaining skill in evaluating them. This claim implies that evaluation is the more difficult skill. Why might this be?

In constructing an argument to support a claim of our own, we already accept the claim as true. We believe it or we wouldn't be bothering to argue for it. In evaluating another's argument in support of a claim, this is not necessarily the case. We may believe the claim is entirely wrong. Asked to evaluate an argument in this circumstance, students, and indeed all of us, find it hard not to be influenced by our own position. When people agree with the arguer that the claim is true, they have an easier time. They can simply identify with the arguer and evaluate the strength of the supporting arguments and evidence as if the claim were their own. When they do not believe the claim is true, they face a more challenging task. They must temporarily set aside their own contrary belief regarding the claim in order to focus on and evaluate how well the claimant supports it.

This reasoning about reasoning—a form of *metacognition*—is difficult for students to master. Thus, a common response by middle-schoolers asked to choose the stronger of two arguments is to choose the one whose claim they agree with, offering as a justification, "This is a good argument, because what it claims is true."

When the evaluator confuses the claim and the argument, the argument itself gets ignored. This error is most serious when evaluators dismiss an argument because they don't endorse the claim it supports: "It's a bad argument," they say, "because what they're arguing for isn't true."

Here is an example from a study of middle-schoolers.[7] They were asked to evaluate this argument :

Schools should do away with uniforms; they're a bad idea.

Instead of judging this to be a weak (even nonexistent) argument, pointing to the claimant's lack of reasons or evidence to support the claim, many students instead merely oppose the claim itself, stating "That's a bad argument" and often go on to add their own argument for the opposing claim; for example in one student's words:

They are not [a bad idea] because they help you identify students on trips.

This response expresses a coherent reason in support of the opposing claim (uniforms are a good thing). Yet what it does not do is evaluate the strength of the original claimant's argument (which is negligible, since the claimant in fact offers no argument at all to support the claim).

In their reasoning both inside the classroom and in everyday matters outside it, this confusion of claim and argument is an important error students must be helped to avoid. The reason is that it works against their giving any serious attention to points of view they don't agree with. A position can be dismissed as wrong with one fell swoop and the arguments supporting it never considered. In the preceding example, the argument was not developed and there was little to consider. But more often, those we disagree with do have arguments worth considering.

Much of the approach to developing argumentation presented in this book is devoted to getting students deeply engaged in examining claims that (at least initially) they don't agree with. We do this by getting them involved at the outset in arguing with others (and especially others they disagree with), rather than focusing all of their efforts on developing their own arguments or simply on nonfiction reading that acquaints them with others' arguments. Reading about others' views and achieving a superficial acquaintance with them requires a certain level of skill; critically evaluating these views is a decidedly different and higher-level cognitive skill. In the final chapter of this book, we revisit the relations among nonfiction reading, writing, and discussing, and we consider how to achieve the most productive balance among them.

Argument and Argumentation

We have seen by now that when the new Common Core Standards specify that students are to become proficient in producing and evaluating arguments, the skill involved is considerable. Before presenting our approach to developing these skills in Chapters 2 and 3, there is one more critical distinction to make in this introductory chapter. It is the distinction between argument and argumentation. It is an important one for us, as we make the claim that developing students' argument skills should begin with rich, extended practice in argumentation, specifically with their peers.

Whether produced in written or oral form, an argument is normally a static product. It is formulated, usually by a single individual, and thereafter is available for consideration by others. Argumentation, in contrast, is a process. Further, it is a social process, engaged in by at least two people. Their exchange follows certain conventions. The arguers alternate turns and—a very important feature—jointly expect that each will seek both (a) to understand what is being said to them and (b) to be understood by the other. In other words, there exists a joint intentionality when people participate in this very common, everyday form of communication with one another, as well as joint norms that help to fulfill these intentions.

Although we have emphasized its skilled aspects, argumentation as a form of social engagement is not foreign to children. It has strong developmental roots in young children's everyday talk, and these developmental roots are one of its strengths as an educational tool. A parent's firm "No" to a young child may or may not be accompanied by reasons—parents vary greatly in this respect. But within a few years most children will have developed some skill in persuasive argument as a means of achieving their desires in the face of adult objections or in justifying their actions when these are the target of adult disapproval.

As soon as children begin interacting with peers, another form of argumentation emerges. Peer discourse is a discourse form in its own right with its own norms. These norms are not dictated by adults, unless children's interchanges exceed boundaries adults regard as acceptable and children are instructed that they must "talk nice." Most of the time, however, children are left alone to construct their own peer conversations and, along with them, the norms and practices that will characterize this discourse. In this respect, it is distinct from the discourse with adults that takes place at home and in school.

The earliest forms of children's peer discourse are no more complex than the classic exchange:

> **Yes it is.**
>
> **No it isn't.**
>
> **Yes it is.**

Yet even this primitive, seemingly contentless exchange is not without purpose and value. Such dialogs contribute to the developmental objective of recognizing, and eventually coordinating, opposing points of view. Furthermore, they incorporate what we will come to emphasize as a critical attribute of argumentive discourse—the speakers coming to recognize that to advance the dialog they must speak to one another. In other words, the second speaker's utterance is constrained by the need to address what the first speaker has said and to do so in a way that will be comprehensible to this speaker.

If this intentionality is missing, the interchange degenerates into what has been called "collective monologue," in which the two speakers employ their alternating speech as an accompaniment to their own respective activities and purposes. Communication is not an objective. Collective monologue has been characterized by Piaget[8] and others as common among preschool children and a precursor to authentic dialog.

Preschoolers soon replace collective monologues with the "genuine," albeit impoverished, sort of three-turn, three-word-per-turn exchange that appears above. But these do not remain satisfying for long, and peer dialogs, while frequently remaining oppositional, begin to incorporate richer content, with the aim of adding weight to these opposing claims.

The origins of argumentation skill lie in these early developments. In the approach to developing argument skills presented in this book, we seek to take full advantage of these developmental origins. We do so by engaging students, beginning in the middle grades, in dense practice of dialogic argumentation with one another. We claim that doing so constitutes the most productive path to the development of skill in the more traditional forms of argument in academic contexts—in individual expository writing and reading—that have long been the concern of educators and are now greatly emphasized in the new standards.

It will be our obligation in this book to make a case for this claim. We can begin that task here by briefly addressing two questions most likely to be raised. First, don't children already have plenty of opportunity to talk to one another, both in and outside the classroom? Indeed, the goal of many teachers is to get them to do less of this and focus more attention on what their teacher is saying.

In fact, however, observations of classroom life suggest that even in class discussion that occurs in "progressive" classrooms, students most often do little in the way of significant idea exchange. Instead, the teacher is the center and students the spokes of a wheel, as illustrated in the diagram below, with all talk going through the teacher. When students do express their ideas in such class discussions, they typically receive acknowledgment but no meaningful feedback in response to what they have said. The opportunity to speak passes to another student. "Who else wants a turn to say something?" teachers are likely to say to move the discussion along.

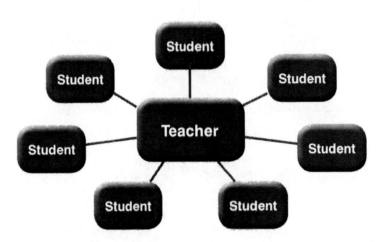

Traditional Classroom Communication Structure

Thus, even dialog between student and teacher is likely to fall short of the sustained exchange of claims and reasons that constitutes authentic intellectual discourse. Instead, the student's main objective is to come up with the response the student thinks the teacher is looking for. Students quickly learn that they are not to argue with their teachers.

In short, most classrooms provide little opportunity for students to engage in serious, sustained dialog with one another, or even with an adult. This is what our curriculum seeks to remedy.

A second question likely to be asked is this: If developing skill in written argument is the educational goal, why not teach it directly, rather than pursuing a seemingly circuitous route through discourse? We address this question more fully later. For now, we note simply that students may find essay writing hard in large part because they do not see the point of it. If so, dialogic argumentation becomes a remedy able to provide the "missing interlocutor" that gives written argument a point.[9] Conversation has a naturalness and, most of all, a purpose that essay writing cannot match. Hence, serious, focused discourse can serve as a bridge between talking and writing. Later in the book, we note the results of our studies comparing the effects of discourse-focused versus writing-focused approaches on students' argumentive writing. First, we turn to a description of our discourse-based approach.

Notes

1. Kuhn, D. (2005). *Education for thinking.* Cambridge: Harvard University Press.

2. National Academies Press (2013). *Education for life and work: Developing transferable knowledge and skills in the 21ˢᵗ century.*

3. Mercier, H., & Sperber, D. (2011). Why do humans reason? Arguments for an argumentative theory. *Behavioral and Brain Sciences, 34,* 57–111; Mercier, H. (2011). Reasoning serves argumentation in children. *Cognitive Development, 26,* 177–191.

4. Oaksford, M., Chater, N., & Hahn, U. (2008). Human reasoning and argumentation: The probabilistic approach. In J. Adler & L. Rips (Eds.), *Reasoning: Studies of human inference and its foundations.* New York: Cambridge University Press. p. 383.

5. Kuhn, D., Wang, Y., & Li, H. (2011). Why argue? Developing understanding of the purposes and value of argumentive discourse. *Discourse Processes, 48,* 26–49.

6. Baum, L., Danovitch, J., & Keil, F. (2008). Children's sensitivity to circular explanations. *Journal of Experimental Child Psychology, 100,* 146–155.

7. Kuhn, D., Zillmer, N, Crowell, A., & Zavala, J. (2013). Developing norms of argumentation: Metacognitive, epistemological, and social dimensions of developing argumentive competence. *Cognition & Instruction, 31,* 456–496.

8. Piaget, J. (1962). *The language and thought of the child.* London: Routledge and Kegan Paul.

9. Graff, G. (2003). *Clueless in academe: How schooling obscures the life of the mind.* New Haven: Yale University Press.

Chapter 2

■ ■ ■

The Curriculum in Broad View

IN THIS CHAPTER WE INTRODUCE THE RATIONALE UNDERLYING THE CURRICULUM and its key characteristics. What makes it distinctive? What is it able to deliver?

Where Do Students Begin?

Despite the roots in early conversation that we noted in Chapter 1, and contrary to what some parents might claim, young adolescents are by no means natural-born arguers. They may be prone to argue, but they fall far short of exercising the skills of accomplished debaters. A lawyer in the courtroom or debater at a tournament presents his or her position in the strongest, most persuasive way possible, yet devotes equal attention to the opposing position and seeks ways to weaken it. Our studies of middle-school students arguing with a peer on significant issues reveals a quite different and decidedly less effective strategy.

These beginning debaters are well aware their opponents disagree with them, and they may work doggedly to "win" the argument. But the strategy they typically deploy is to ignore their opponent's position and its supporting arguments. Instead, all of their attention is devoted to their own position. They may even listen respectfully to the opponent. But when the turn to speak returns to them, they resume their mission to showcase their own side, each time more emphatically and perhaps with more elaboration. For these young debaters, the objective is to get their own ideas delivered more forcefully and they hope more powerfully, allowing them to prevail. The opponent's position, meanwhile, they see as simply fading away as less worthy, even though it remains unexamined. The exchange shown at the top of the next page captures this approach.

Verbal, outgoing students assume this "my side only" stance quite comfortably when first asked to debate with a peer. But the argumentation skills of other students start out at an even less advanced level. These students are not accustomed to expressing their views, and if called upon to do so, they respond with no more than a word or two of agreement or disagreement. Such students—and there are many—have rarely been asked what they think about a serious issue, in or outside of school, and they do not expect to be held accountable for what they think about anything. Being asked to take a position on a serious issue is a new experience for them, and it can be hard at first to elicit much more than the response shown below.

It will take students who start at this level some time and encouragement to become comfortable in formulating and expressing their ideas—to become used to being listened to and to having what they say taken seriously. In many classrooms, students may have at least occasional opportunities to express a view, but most often it is merely acknowledged, rather than engaged. The teacher says, "Thanks for sharing your idea, Tim; who else has an idea to share?"

Yet we have found that with time and practice, most students find that they like being listened to. Furthermore, the experience motivates them to undertake the hard work of developing and better articulating their ideas. Wherever students' starting points, the goal we have for all of them is depicted in the following exchange.

What Skills Do We Want to Develop?

Although entry points are likely to vary, depending on how accustomed a student is to expressing an opinion and expecting it to be taken seriously, the developmental goals are the same. These are summarized in Table 2-1. These goals, together with the kind of student activities that support each goal, form a curriculum roadmap. It shapes many of the specifics that we present in Chapter 3.

Table 2-1. Summary of Curriculum Activities and Associated Cognitive Goals

CURRICULUM ACTIVITY	COGNITIVE GOAL
Generating reasons	Reasons underlie opinions. Different reasons exist for the same opinion.
Elaborating reasons	Good reasons support opinions.
Evaluating reasons	Some reasons are better than others.
Developing reasons into an argument	Reasons connect to one another and are building blocks of argument.
Examining and evaluating opponents' reasons	Opponents have reasons too.
Generating counterarguments to others' reasons	Reasons may have flaws and can be countered.
Generating rebuttals to others' counterarguments	Counters to reasons can be rebutted.
Supporting [and weakening] arguments with evidence	Evidence can strengthen claims. It can also weaken claims.
Contemplating mixed evidence	The same evidence can be used to support or weaken different claims. The same claim can be supported or weakened by different pieces of evidence.
Conducting and evaluating two-sided arguments	Opposing positions must be weighed in a framework of alternatives and evidence.
Constructing a [written or oral] individual argument	An individual argument can be constructed from a dialogic argument.

The sequence in Table 2-1 isn't one that students progress through in a strict order, moving on to the next objective only after a previous one is mastered. Rather, students cycle through this progression many times over with new and different and gradually more complex ideas and topics. Still, some objectives are more fundamental than others and need to be addressed first. Following are key questions students need to ask themselves (and one another).

Ask: Why Do I Think So?

A first, most fundamental step, as seen in Table 2-1, is for students to recognize that opinions have reasons. Opinions, if they are to be taken seriously, become positions or claims that then need reasons to support them. As the box below illustrates, reasons supporting a position can differ, and two people can hold the same position for many different reasons. Furthermore, as students begin to realize once they think and talk about them, some reasons are better than others.

Shall We Do It?

Yes, but I don't know why.
Yes, because it's the only solution to the problem.
Yes, because it's the safest solution to the problem.
Yes, because other solutions are riskier.
Yes, because it's the best solution in the short run.
Yes, because it's the best solution in the long run.

Recognizing that all reasons are not equal motivates the hard conceptual work of examining reasons closely and evaluating them. Getting just to this point is a significant developmental benchmark. It is one that takes some time to reach, as students gain practice articulating and supporting their positions on an issue and evaluating their own and others' reasons. What makes some reasons better than others as support for a claim? Answering this question paves the way for the goal of fashioning the best reasons into a comprehensive argument. How do these different reasons relate to one another? Which ones best connect to one another to make the strongest argument in support of our position?

Ask: What Does the Other Side Say?

Oh...he's thinking about this too!

Once these building blocks are in place, the next challenge is the one we identified at the outset of this chapter: Students must come to recognize that opponents have their own reasons and arguments, possibly even powerful ones, for holding the position they do. These demand fully as much consideration as one's own reasons and arguments.

With the experience of engaging deeply with peers whose views differ that our curriculum provides, students do achieve this recognition. It has two potential benefits:

- Attending to opposing arguments and giving them careful thought are the first steps toward developing ways to challenge them.

- Doing so helps to clarify the thinking that underlies one's own position.

Undertaking to weaken an opponent's argument—called *counterargument*—is a central objective of skilled argumentation. Of course one's own arguments are vulnerable to counterargument as well, but rebuttals—counterarguments to a counterargument—can potentially restore their strength. Counterargument and rebuttal, we see in the next chapter, play a central role in argumentation and in our curriculum. A first and essential step in mastering these cognitive tools is to recognize that those who disagree with us have their own ideas. These ideas may be as good as or even better than ours, but in any case they demand close examination. This is the recognition that lays the ground for genuine dialog, which allows two opposing views to intersect and ideally, in the process, create a richer understanding on both sides.

Ask: How Do We Know?

Evidence is central to argument. It is what we turn to in order to answer the question "How do we know?". Weakening another's argument through counterargument very often entails critiquing the evidence on which it rests. Rational discourse assumes and demands a respect for evidence. Evidence serves two potential functions:

- As a source of support for one's own argument

- As a means of weakening an opposing argument

We do not emphasize the role of evidence early in the curriculum, giving students the opportunity to first focus on the more fundamental challenge of listening to and addressing one another in authentic argumentive discourse. Once we do begin to focus on evidence, however, it assumes a critical role. Thinking about evidence is intellectually demanding because it entails thinking about thinking, or *metacognition*. Evidence serves as a reason for a reason: It supports the reason I have given to justify my position, just as it serves this same function for an opponent. Equally important, evidence can serve to weaken, rather than support, a position.

The role of evidence is particularly crucial in the context of argumentive discourse, when positions, and their supporting reasons, are opposed. A debate between opposing views may well rest on evidence. Evidence is central to argument because it is shared and cannot be ignored. More so than reasons, which are our own intellectual constructions, evidence to a much greater extent exists "out there" for consumption by all as statements of "the way things are."

Hmm...How do I know this??

Still, regarding evidence as "just the facts, ma'am" is an oversimplification and misleading. "Facts" can end up meaning quite different things depending on how they are framed and put to use. We can draw on the same statistics to talk about the percentage of lives saved by a certain medical procedure or the percentage of lives lost and derive quite different implications.

Evidence can of course be questioned as to its accuracy. But evidence cannot be ignored, except at great risk to the soundness of our argument. It is there for parties on both sides of an issue to make use of as they wish. We cannot address an opponent's argument effectively without bringing to bear on it all of the relevant evidence. Nor can we be in command of our own arguments unless we are sure of the evidence supporting them, i.e., how we know what we know.

From Debate to Exposition

As depicted below, thinking cannot be seen as residing exclusively within individual minds or in the interchanges between those minds. But practice in the social sphere can eventually transfer to the individual sphere. Our curriculum serves as a path from argumentive discourse to individual argumentive writing or speaking. The forms of dialog students have engaged in become robust enough to be interiorized within an individual mind. The dialog then becomes expressible by this individual in an integrated form, either written or spoken. Unlike the "my side only" arguments depicted earlier, however, such arguments integrate and address opposing perspectives, in a framework of reasons and evidence for and against each. In Chapter 4, we visit this progress in detail, examining how students' individual argumentive writing develops over time during the course of the dense experience in dialogic argument afforded by our curriculum.

Where Does Thinking Reside?

The single most important claim we make in this book is the one we have just made—that rich practice in dialogic argumentation with peers is a fruitful path to the development of skill in the more traditional forms of argument—notably, individual expository writing—emphasized in school and critical to academic achievement beyond the early grades. The dialogic nature of our curriculum is thus its single most important characteristic. However, there are others that we now turn to.

Distinctive Features of the Curriculum

Having previewed its objectives, we turn to the curriculum itself. We begin by describing it in terms of its broad characteristics, and we convey the rationale for each of these features—not just what we do, but why. In Chapter 3, we turn to more specific description of the sequence of activities that comprise the curriculum.

Community: What Do We Do Here?

A major feature of the curriculum is its social frame. We do not conceive of our objective narrowly as one of developing individual cognitive skills. As the sketch above highlights, thinking is a social activity, not just an individual one. Argumentation by definition takes place in a social context. This context is central to developing individual skill. Hence, even if individual competencies are seen as the ultimate goal, it is the social context of a community that we claim is central to achieving them. Schools are indeed such communities, and within a school exist many smaller communities that students themselves define and are in turn defined by.

Those who participate in a community defined by shared activities come to share a set of standards and values that support engaging in those activities. In the case of argumentive discourse, participants must have the disposition and will, as well as the skills, to argue. They must see the point of doing so. These are dispositions and values that develop largely through socialization in an environment that supports them. Only through sustained participation in activities and settings that "expect such behavior, support it, and reward it in overt and subtle ways"[1] do students come to truly appreciate reasoned discourse. Furthermore, the claims they make to one another come to be based on shared standards of knowing. These standards come to be valued as worthy of upholding and expected of all who would enter the conversation. Criticism becomes the likely consequence of violations. They adopt what Resnick et al.[1] call "accountable talk." Our curriculum creates such a community of shared expectations among its participants.

Goals: Why Are We Doing It?

Another feature of the curriculum is its goal-based structure. Goal-based activities make it possible for students to see a specific purpose in what they are doing—something too often missing in what students do in school. The peer discourse we engage students in has a goal that they can recognize and will appreciate when it has been achieved. This is so even though their understanding of the goal is only partial at the outset and evolves over time. Initially the goal is one of preparing for and winning a final debate (the "Showdown") with the team who holds the opposing position. With time, however, the focus on winning diminishes and students become interested in the quality of the argumentation. They strive to construct strong counterarguments and rebuttals as an end in itself. They want not just to win but to produce strong arguments, ones they anticipate their opponents won't be able to easily "shoot down."

With time the emphasis further shifts from the Showdown debate as the culminating activity to a final essay that students write individually at the conclusion of each debate topic. They will have engaged with their peers in examining the topic for a dozen or more class periods over a number of weeks, and they come to feel entitled to now produce a position piece that conveys their own conclusions and the thinking behind them.

Accountability: How Are We Doing?

The objective of students becoming accountable to one another is supported by the fact that the activities that constitute the curriculum center around peer interchange, rather than whole-class, teacher-directed talk. As the core activity of the curriculum, students argue electronically with a series of peers who have taken an opposing position on a controversial issue. Students are thus constantly on call, needing to respond to one another's contributions to the dialog. In whole-class discussion, in sharp contrast, students can fade in and out, raising a hand now and then when motivated to do so, the rest of the time assuming the passive role of audience.

We organize the activity such that each student is paired with a same-side peer; as a pair they debate a series of opposing-side pairs. This makes students accountable in multiple ways—to the same-side peer and to the opposing-side pair. With every exchange they are called upon to hold up their end of the dialog, in accordance with evolving group norms as to what constitutes accountable talk.

Visibility: Representing and Reflecting on What Happens

Another of our goals is to support students' thinking by making it more visible. Doing so increases their awareness of their own and others' thinking, a first step in enabling them to reflect on it, and, in so doing, to enrich it. We achieve this objective in a number of ways. The most distinctive of these is that students conduct most of their discourse electronically, making use of instant-messaging software that serves this function. The written transcript of the dialog that the software provides gives students the opportunity to review and reflect on what has been said. This feature stands in striking contrast to face-to-face dialog, where the spoken word disappears as soon as it is uttered, challenging memory capacities. In addition to serving as a reference point and framework during the dialogs, the transcripts become the object of various reflective activities that students engage in.

The familiarity that most students will have with electronic media facilitates their use of the method. Yet we have not chosen to use it simply because students like it and it's the medium of today. Rather, we have adopted it because of what it can do to support the thinking that students bring to it. Representing ideas in concrete, visible form enhances students' ability to reflect on and work with them.

Questioning: What Do We Know?

In their discourse with one another, students will not be able to generate rich arguments and counterarguments in a vacuum. They need to bring information relevant to the topic to inform their reasoning. Depending on the topic, they will likely already have some degree of related knowledge that they are ready to summon to support their arguments (or to weaken those of their opponents). But much relevant knowledge they will not have.

One approach we might take is to ask students to begin their work on a topic by reading material about it that they can then draw on in their argumentation. A problem with this approach is that students don't yet appreciate the purpose that this information serves. In a word, it provides answers to questions they don't yet have. As a result they fail to see its point. They are thus likely to approach such reading disinterestedly, as just another reading assignment to be completed and most likely forgotten.

A small dose of initial reading can be productive, to heighten initial interest in the topic, but at the outset we employ it sparingly out of concern that a deluge of information up front not only is met with disinterest but can shut down students' own inquisitiveness about a topic. Therefore, we let students' own ideas dominate at the beginning of their engagement with a new topic, encouraging them to articulate and share with one another their ideas about the topic. And, we have found, they do have lots of ideas to share, even in the case of topics outside the range of their immediate experience that we might expect them to know little about.

Still, students' discourse stands to be informed and enriched by information related to the topic, information that in most cases will be new to them. Rather than making a large body of information available to students at once, however, we have found it more effective to create a need for the information they acquire. It can then be made available to them on this "as needed" basis. Hence, rather than provide answers to questions students don't have, we let them first formulate the questions. In this way, we allow students to first see how such information could be useful in achieving the objectives they have set for themselves, before we assist them in securing it.

After introducing a few basic questions regarding the topic, and making answers available, we thus invite students to submit questions of their own, the answers to which they think might be useful to them in their argumentation on the topic. At the next session, we then make available brief factual answers to these questions (which sometimes students assist in obtaining), and the resulting question-and-answer "evidence set" becomes a document available for use by the entire class.

The objective is for students not just to acquire information but to see its value and therefore be disposed to apply it. It is in this dispositional potential that we see our method as a powerful one. With practice, we have found, students do in fact in time make extensive use of such information in their argumentation, coming to recognize it as playing the critical role of evidence serving to strengthen their own arguments or weaken those of their opponents.

In the contemporary climate of the Common Core Standards, in which gaining information from nonfiction sources has been prioritized as a critical academic skill, we see this question-generating approach as a powerful method of strengthening students' skills in processing new factual information. No better way can be laid for the acquisition of new knowledge than for it to fill a gap that the learner himself or herself has identified.

Reflection: Thinking It Over

Because students work in pairs in conducting an electronic dialog with an opposing pair, they must agree in advance on what to communicate to the opposing pair. This essentially doubles the participation in reasoned discourse (both verbal within the same-side pair and electronic between opposing pairs). Doing so provides an opportunity for metacognitive planning and reflection (since the pair must reflect on the opponents' statements and debate what to say to them in return). Fostering this reflective, or metacognitive, aspect of argumentive competence, we believe, is an important factor in the success of the method. Planning and evaluating are key metacognitive activities, and students get intensive practice in them, in a context of their own goal-based and self-directed activity.

Electronic dialogs are supplemented by activities based on the dialogs that function as additional tools of reflection. Illustrated in the next chapter, these reflective activities ask students to identify strong and weak arguments and their counterarguments and rebuttals, as well as relevant evidence. They remain available as resources during preparation for the final Showdown and the Showdown itself, as well as the debrief analysis that follows.

These reflective activities also serve another, more subtle purpose. By documenting their ideas in writing—their arguments, evidence, counterarguments, and rebuttals—students are encouraged to commit to them, to take ownership of them. These written artifacts thus serve as another way of conveying to students that they are responsible for what they say—that they are engaging in accountable talk.

Flexibility: Time Scale and Students

We are now almost ready to turn to a detailed description of the 13-class sequence of sessions that constitutes the curriculum. The sequence is devoted to a single topic. It begins with small-group, same-side team work ("Pre-Game") and proceeds to paired electronic dialogs with the opposing side ("Game"). Final small-group preparation precedes a whole-class "Showdown" debate that serves as the capstone experience ("End-Game"), followed by a debrief session and a final individual essay assignment on the topic. By the end of the sequence, students have engaged deeply with the topic and are very familiar with it.

Before describing the sequence in detail in the next chapter, it is important to emphasize the considerable flexibility of the curriculum. Flexibility applies both to the kinds of student populations who stand to benefit from participation and to the time frame for such participation, as well as the wide choice of topics.

With respect to time frame, we recognize that their particular circumstances will allow few teachers or schools, initially in any case, to adopt the curriculum as an extended two-year sequence, as we portray it in the next chapters. We describe a 13-session sequence devoted to a single topic, with the potential to be repeated multiple times with new topics. In our own work with the curriculum, we have engaged students with multiple topics over two and occasionally three academic years, devoting two class sessions per week, over about seven weeks, to each topic. In later chapters, we describe the progress that students show over this period, both during the course of the curriculum itself and in assessments of their skills following the curriculum, comparing them to the skills of closely matched non-participating students.

Teachers can nonetheless observe benefits of the program in a single sequence, devoted to one topic. The topic can be one they choose to best fit their own curricula, or it can be chosen from the list of suggestions we provide. The sequence fits appropriately within an ELA, social studies, or science curriculum. Individual sessions can take place daily for several weeks as a concentrated unit. Or, in the form we have employed it most often, sessions can occur twice weekly over a period of six to seven weeks. This makes it possible to fit two sequences, for two different topics, into a semester and four topics into an academic year. Another delivery model we have recently begun to explore is to present the 13 sessions devoted to a topic in concentrated fashion over two to three days, in the form of a workshop or summer institute. Students attending such an event for a full week likely will be able to complete two topics.

The curriculum is suitable for all kinds of students across a wide age and ability range from middle elementary grades through high school. The complexity of the topics and materials students work with can vary so as to be suited to different student populations. The curriculum can be productive with students of widely varying ability levels and academic backgrounds. Students in academically advantaged schools may not find it as different from other project-based work they have engaged in as will students from academically disadvantaged schools, and in part for this reason we believe it is a particularly beneficial activity for the latter, disadvantaged group. The concern has been voiced that instruction for such students focuses only on so-called "basic skills" and the potential for such students to exercise higher-order thinking skills is neglected. Our curriculum is one that such students can readily engage in, and one in which we have demonstrated that they make significant progress with respect to higher-order thinking.

Topics: What's Worth Talking About?

The curriculum allows teachers and students the flexibility of deciding on their own topics, and teachers may want to tailor topics to coordinate with particular units in their own curricula. We have found it useful, especially with less experienced and initially less articulate students, to begin with topics close to students' own experience. The possibilities for such introductory topics are many. These are two we have used successfully many times:

- Should misbehaving students be expelled or given a second chance?

- Should parents be allowed to home-school their child?

Once students get accustomed to the method, we then move on to topics of broader scope. Four we have found very productive are these:

- Should animals be used in research?

- Should human organ sales be allowed?

- Are teen offenders best tried in adult or juvenile court?

- Is China's one-child policy justifiable?

In the appendices at the end of the book, we provide illustrative supporting materials for the topics we have mentioned, and suggest many other potential topics. In the second year of the curriculum, we have typically offered students an opportunity to generate their own topic ideas and choose ones to debate. Interestingly, in two consecutive years in multiple classrooms, the topic that received the greatest interest and majority vote has been abortion, and some of the illustrative material in Chapter 3 features students' debate of this topic.

Notes

1.   Resnick, L.B., Michaels, S., & O'Connor, C. (2010). How (well structured) talk builds the mind. In R. Sternberg & D. Preiss (Eds.), *From genes to context: New discoveries about learning from educational research and their applications.* New York: Springer. p. 172.

Chapter 3

■ ■ ■

The Curriculum Session by Session

I
N THIS CHAPTER WE TURN TO A SESSION-BY-SESSION DESCRIPTION of the curriculum sequence for a given topic. In addition to describing specific activities and objectives for each session, we provide video clips that allow these to come alive for readers, illustrating both the teacher's role in introducing the activities and guiding the students' work and the students' roles in engaging these activities. (An icon next to the text indicates an accompany video; see Preface for access instructions.) Relevant Common Core Standards are noted in relation to specific activities. Finally, as an aide to implementation, in an appendix at the end of the book we provide "nuts and bolts" procedural guides separately for the first-year and second-year curriculum, as their activities differ somewhat for some sessions. Refer to these guides for more details on the activities described in this chapter, supporting materials for classroom use, and tips and options to help ensure that things go smoothly in the classroom.

Both the descriptions in this chapter and the appendix curriculum guides should be taken as suggestive, rather than prescriptive. Teachers who wish to introduce a version of this curriculum in their classrooms will each have their own set of circumstances, objectives, styles, and preferences that will shape their implementation. The flexibility of the curriculum enables teachers and their students to take ownership of the curriculum and make it their own.

The 13-session sequence per topic remains largely the same across the first and second year of the curriculum. The main difference between the first and second years is one of focus. The first year curriculum focuses on the basic objective of getting students to engage one another's ideas, at first merely by paying attention to them and then through effective generation and use of counterarguments and rebuttals. The second year focuses on the critical role of skilled use of evidence to strengthen and weaken claims. By the end of the first year and throughout the second year, evidence related to the topic is introduced explicitly. Students are encouraged to generate questions, the answers to which they think might be useful to them in their argumentation on the topic. The resulting question-and-answer "evidence set" then becomes a shared document available for use by the entire class. Use of this document is the major feature that differentiates the second year curriculum from the first.

Teachers will want to use their discretion as to when students are ready to move on to the second-year curriculum, with its focus on evidence. It could be as early as the middle of the first year or not until the middle of the second year. Thus, rather than present the two years separately, in this chapter we describe a single sequence that characterizes both years, while in the more-detailed appendix curriculum guides, the year 1 and year 2 sequences are presented separately for ease in classroom use.

Introducing the Curriculum

Introducing students to the curriculum and engaging their interest in what they will be doing and why is a crucial initial step before embarking on the activities themselves. It is unlikely that students will have previously experienced an extended sequence of activities on a single topic like the one they are about to engage in. The curriculum is more student-centered than they are likely used to, and their teacher's role as coach rather than traditional teacher requires some getting used to by both teachers and students. Also there are some new understandings to be introduced and misconceptions that need to be corrected, such as argument as something to be avoided.

The most crucial new understanding students need to achieve at the outset is that they are learning skills, rather than a particular body of content knowledge. Because they will be thinking and talking a lot about very specific topics, this understanding will take some time and effort to fully develop and will be subject to mis-conception. Students today are used to being tested regularly on specific bodies of knowledge, and after the first topic cycle is completed they may even ask "What do we need to know about this?" They may not yet recognize that their learning extends far beyond the specific topics they address.

We therefore recommend an initial discussion introducing students to the curriculum, the goals or outcomes they are expected to achieve, and the roles that they and the adults involved will play. In such a discussion, five key points deserve emphasis:

- Unexamined beliefs are not worth having. Opinions without reasons are worth little. To hold a position demands being accountable for it, to ourselves and others, and that requires having sound, strong arguments for what we believe. At the same time we must be willing to change what we believe, replacing old beliefs with new ones, as we learn more and our earlier belief no longer seems justified.

- Rather than being bad or to be avoided, arguing, done the correct way, is a good thing. It is a powerful way of communicating with one another about important issues, clarifying what we think about them, and reaching sound conclusions and decisions. Arguing not only helps us understand what others think about the issue, it helps us better understand what we ourselves think. No less a wise man than Socrates said that until you argue about it with others you don't really know what you think about something. Those who disagree with us introduce us to what we haven't thought of, and those who agree help us to think through our position more fully and more deeply.

- The goal of engaging in argumentation with another person who disagrees with us is not to shoot down and destroy the other person's ideas, but rather to engage these ideas, think carefully about them, and learn from them. Both of the participants in argumentation should come out richer from the experience.

- When we critique another person's ideas, it is important to remember that it is only the ideas that we are questioning and possibly criticizing. It is never the person. Very competent, worthy people often have ideas that don't hold up under scrutiny. The moral is, judge the idea, not the person.

- Arguing is something we begin doing early in life. But arguing well involves skills that must be developed. Like athletic or musical skills, they are best learned by consistent, thoughtful practice, both individually and with others. Improving skills requires time and effort.

If appropriate, you may want to share some of these ideas with students in written form, such as shown in the box below. This written summary can also be shared with parents when presenting the curriculum to them on parents' nights. Parents may initially be skeptical about nontraditional investment of students' time; it will be helpful to explain that the skills emphasized in the curriculum are skills their children will need in their high school and college work and increasingly in 21st-century careers. Students themselves, however, may play the greater role in convincing parents of the value of this curriculum: Students, we have found, often bring home the issues they discuss in a curriculum like ours and engage their parents in dinner-table conversations that benefit all.

In addition to reassuring parents as to the value of this nontraditional use of classroom time, even more critical is student "buy-in." Students find the program initially novel and engaging and with little encouragement are happy to take on their assignment. As the sequence proceeds, they benefit from the momentum building up to a finale. It is the deeper buy-in that is ultimately important, however, as their objectives gradually shift from their team winning the final Showdown debate to displaying their skills—which they do with their teammates by developing arguments that withstand critique, weakening their opponents' arguments, and channeling this experience into the culminating and more traditional activity of writing their own individual final-position essays. Initially, this final activity seems superfluous to them ("Why do we have to write an essay after we already have a Showdown winner?"). By the end, they are likely to agree that these essays are indeed the most notable product of their work on the topic. Toward this end, the points emphasized here and in the class description can profitably be revisited with students from time to time as they engage the curriculum.

Sample Class Description for Students and Parents

In this class, you will engage with classmates in some deep thinking about contemporary social issues and enduring philosophical ones. A central objective is to develop intellectual skills, ones that are critical if you are to prosper in your remaining school years and beyond. Intellectual skills are like athletic or musical skills in that they are developed by consistent practice. No one can show them or tell them to you while you sit back and listen. In this course you need to have "minds on," doing something, 100 percent of the time. There is no sitting back and listening. It's hard work, just like developing athletic skill, but it's the only way.

This class also differs from others in that you can't simply give back answers on a test to show that you've learned certain things. Because we will do the same kinds of activities repeatedly with new topics, you can't write down a list each week of "here's what I learned." You may even wonder whether you have learned anything at all. But we will measure how your skills are developing with weekly dedicated practice, similar to the way athletic skills develop with continued practice. Your job is to keep up the hard work and realize you are learning something important even if you can't explain it as easily as you can in your other classes.

Your grade will be based on your written work and on class participation, including contributing to small-group work and participation in "Showdowns." Half of your grade will be based on class work, including written assignments, collaborative work with classmates, and participation in the final Showdown for each topic. The other half of your grade will be based on a final individual essay for the topic in the form of a Letter to the Editor.

Getting Started —
Session Outline for Teachers

Pre-Game Phase: Developing Reasons into Arguments (Sessions 1 & 2)

Overview: What happens in the Pre-Game phase?

• Students assemble into pro and con teams based on the opinions they've given on the topic.

• In small groups, teams share and develop reasons that support their position.

• Students evaluate and revise reasons.

• Students consider evidence to connect to their reasons (year 2).

Pre-Game Phase: Links to Key Competencies from Common Core State Standards

• Initiate and participate effectively in a range of collaborative discussions (one-on-one, in groups, and teacher-led) with diverse partners on grades 9–10 topics, texts, and issues, building on others' ideas and expressing their own clearly and persuasively. [SL.9-10.1]

• Write arguments to support claims with clear reasons and relevant evidence. [W.6.1]

• Delineate and evaluate the argument and specific claims in a text, assessing whether the reasoning is sound and the evidence is relevant and sufficient; recognize when irrelevant evidence is introduced. [RI.8.8]

Pre-Game Phase: Links to Key Competencies from Next Generation Science Standards

• Support an argument with evidence, data, or a model. [5-PS2-1, 5-ESS1-1]

• Construct and present oral and written arguments supported by empirical evidence and scientific reasoning to support or refute an explanation or a model for a phenomenon or a solution to a problem. [MS-PS2-4]

Taking a Position

Many young adolescent students, as we noted in Chapter 2, will have very little experience with being asked what they think about something and expecting to be listened to. At most they will be accustomed to expressing personal tastes and preferences—about a music group or fashion trend—and even in these cases they are not used to having to defend their positions. It's not important to them to justify why one group "has it" and another is out, and it's perfectly acceptable for such views to change repeatedly, with little if any explanation given or expected. This is the starting point for many students, and building from it occurs slowly but steadily.

When we first ask middle-school students to take a position on a substantive issue, we therefore must expect that it is not a deeply held position and that only with considerable effort and practice will they develop a cohesive, well-founded argument capable of supporting this position within a framework of its alternatives. Understanding that their classmates on the other side of the room have taken an opposing view is a catalyst in initiating this understanding. "How can they think that?" leads to the question, "Why do we think this?"

The path to this understanding, we believe, is a social one. It is critical that students get used to being listened to by their peers and sensing that their views are respected and valued—that they genuinely have something to say. We thus ask students to take a position and then in collaboration with like-minded peers, to develop a justifiable commitment to it. It is critical at this early point to establish a climate of respect for individuals and for ideas. "Criticize Ideas, Not People" is a motto we have displayed prominently in classrooms while students are engaged in our curriculum. All ideas deserve to be heard and the contributor of the idea deserves to be respected even if we disagree with the idea. Only through the group's thinking carefully about ideas can conclusions be reached about which ones are better than others.

Although most of the features of the curriculum are flexible, one that we urge users to adopt is to allow students to choose their own side of an issue, rather than be assigned to one. Arbitrary assignment and the experience of debating both sides of an issue are common in more advanced forms of debate practiced by high school and college debate teams. But to begin, young students should see that there is nothing arbitrary about the reasons they are generating and arguments they are building. The thinking they are doing to support a position is genuine, not an exercise. Real people in the real world have real beliefs that they need or want to justify and these are ways they do it.

As they engage the topic, students may decide they have chosen the wrong side and wish to change. We have found this happens infrequently, but there is no reason it can't be accommodated in the early segments of the sequence. Also, there are likely to be students who decline to take an initial position, selecting "undecided" or "uncertain" in the initial opinion poll. Assignment of these students to one side or the other can be useful in maintaining a balance in size between the pro and con teams.

Generating Reasons: Why Do We Think This?

Once opinions have been solicited and the two sides formed, each side assembles separately, ideally in separate rooms but more likely at opposite ends of their classroom. Each side is further divided, arbitrarily, into an A and a B team, which, depending on total class size, will consist of six to eight students each. Ideally, an adult coach is available for each side (e.g., the class teacher and assistant), as this adult can then in the eyes of the students become identified with the group and their position (although not explicitly endorsing it). In other words, the coach becomes an advocate of the group and its objectives (as distinguished from an advocate of the position as his or her own). If a second adult is not available to participate, however, a single classroom teacher can function in this role for both sides, being careful to maintain an attitude of neutrality.

Generating initial reasons. Teams can temporarily break down further into two small groups of three or four each (thus four small groups per side) if class size warrants. Each group has a supply of large index cards and each student is asked to write their most important reason for taking the position they have. "We need to get these reasons out on the table and decide what we think of them," the coach suggests in initiating the activity. Students work silently completing this initial activity. At first, some students may need encouragement in generating and expressing a reason.

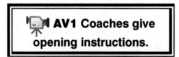
AV1 Coaches give opening instructions.

In this initial phase of the curriculum, "adult talk" is likely to dominate, as coaches give instructions for each activity and provide clarification and individual help as needed. This changes, however, once students become familiar with the sequence of activities that repeat for each new topic. In the accompanying video clips, we include brief excerpts both of adult coaches giving instructions and of students carrying out the activities (with the exception of the initial activity, where students work silently). We also often include excerpts of instructions as presented by two different coaches to different classes, to provide a sense of the variability of the different personalities and styles the coaches bring to their role. There is no single right way to fulfill the coach role.

Thinking about reasons. Once each student in the group has generated at least one reason, students pass their cards to the student on the left, who is asked to read and think about it, asking the writer to explain if needed. The receiving student is then asked to rewrite the reason, below the original, using fewer words: "Keep the main point but make it quicker and easier to read later." Students then take turns reading their "fewer words" version of their neighbor's reason to the group. The original writer must agree with the fewer-words version and all members of the group must understand the reason and agree that this is the best way to express it. Once approved, the short version is circled and the card put on display in the middle of the table. The main purpose of the "fewer words" task is to get students to think deeply about the reason and what it is really saying.

This procedure is then repeated for the next student, with the presenting student acting as spokesperson for the neighbor's reason, until all cards have been addressed. An addition after the first card is that when the card is placed in the middle of the table, the group compares it to the card(s) already there, asking, "Is it the same reason as one already there or a different one?" If it's judged the same, it's fastened to the original reason card, leaving on top the card that the group agrees expresses the reason the best.

AV2 Students are instructed on how to share their reasons, have peers interpret them, reduce each unique reason to its best "fewer words" version, and eliminate any duplicates.

Figure 3-1 illustrates a reason card for the topic of abortion; the fewer-words version the group has agreed on is circled. We have chosen abortion as the topic for this illustration, as well as for a number of the video clips, in order to show how well students are able to do with a complex, difficult topic that some might consider inappropriate for this age group. Interestingly, when we solicit ideas from students of topics they would like to debate, abortion repeatedly appears at the top of the list.

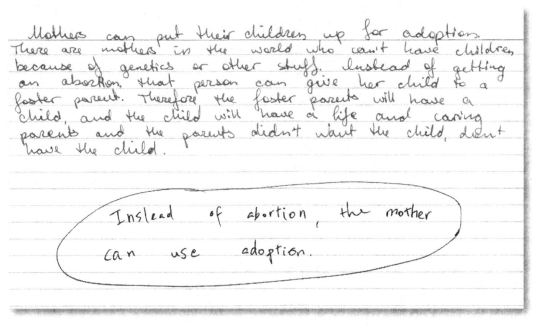

Figure 3-1. Sample Reason Card for Abortion Topic

An optional activity near the end of session 1 (depending on time remaining in the class session) is for the two groups that make up each team to combine and repeat this procedure, with the objective of eliminating duplicates and assembling a final set of reasons for the whole team. If time permits, teams might take a preliminary vote on which is their strongest reason. A final optional activity for this first session is to assign students the task of soliciting additional reasons to bring to the next class.

AV3 Two student groups carry out session 1 activities.

These activities typically conclude session 1. However, this dividing point is arbitrary, and some classes may not finish the preceding activities in one session. In these cases it is better to have the activities extend into session 2 than conclude them prematurely, with the objective of at least each group having a completed, agreed-on, set of reason cards. Further elimination of duplicates can be achieved later.

The preceding activities are vehicles to promote students' reflecting, individually and jointly, on reasons. Eliminating duplicate reasons, we have found, is a particularly good vehicle for this purpose as it demands close analysis of each reason's meaning.

Working Further with Reasons: What Makes a Good One?

Optional opening activities for session 2 are to review any new reasons students have brought in and to have teams A and B exchange their reason card sets to review briefly, enabling them to see what their same-side fellow team came up with. Teams get their own reason cards back following this exchange and then have the opportunity to add any reasons they wish.

Evaluating and comparing reasons (year 1). The primary session 2 activity differs in year 1 and year 2. By year 2, students have become focused on attaching evidence to their reasons. In year 1, students benefit from thinking more explicitly about reasons, in particular the concept that some reasons might be better than others and that their reasons need to be organized into an overall argument that takes these differences into account. This activity of examining "reasons for reasons" is one that again has an explicitly reflective, or metacognitive, objective.

For year 1 students, we have found that the activity that best supports this objective is to ask students to sort their reason cards into categories based on merit—best, okay, so-so (or alternative names of their choosing)—following an introductory discussion of the fact that "some reasons are better than others" and the possible criteria for making such judgments (e.g., power to persuade). This initial discussion does not have to be lengthy or definitive, however; better to let students first experience making such judgments themselves, generating their own criteria, and later revisiting the discussion of what criteria should be used.

AV4 Students evaluate and categorize their reasons and look for the best reason.

An alternative to the categorization task is to ask students to do a rank ordering of their set of reasons—although beginning students find this harder. In either case, the group must decide on why a reason belongs where it has been placed. Hence, the group must engage with one another in explicit discussion about the reasons and develop language to justify their evaluative decisions. A conclusion to this activity can be reassembling of the two groups into their full team, so the team as a whole can reconcile their respective efforts and assemble a final set of reason cards in their respective categories. A good objective for this phase is to seek agreement at the team level regarding the reasons that belong in the best category. Ideally (even if not at first), this will lead to some anticipation as to how the reasons will fit together into an overall argumentive strategy for their team. If time, students can be asked to identify their team's very best reason and to think about what role it should play.

Connecting evidence to reasons (year 2). After experience with the first few topic cycles, students will have appropriated their own evaluative stance toward their reasons. They anticipate the progression to the final Showdown, and the role that these reasons will play. Hence, the explicit, structured activity devoted to evaluation can receive less emphasis and be gradually phased out, as students begin to evaluate spontaneously ("How can we use this?"). Classes will vary based on when they reach this point, and a teacher may use discretion in transitioning from the year 1 activity of evaluating reasons to the year 2 activity of connecting evidence to reasons.

Evidence is of course central to argument, but for the first several topic cycles in year 1, we generally do not go beyond having students bring evidence into their arguments spontaneously, allowing them to focus on the more basic year 1 objectives and hopefully to increase their awareness of how evidence might be introduced to strengthen a reason.

At a point in the middle to latter part of year 1 (or later if needed), the role of evidence is introduced more explicitly. It is initially done casually, however, as a potential resource students may want to avail themselves of, rather than as a mandatory activity: "This time we have some evidence available you may want to use to strengthen your arguments." The evidence takes the form of a set of 8 to 10 questions, each printed on a sheet folded to conceal the answer. The set is balanced, with an equal number of Q&A pairs most readily supporting each side and others neutral in this respect. Typically, these are largely ignored at first but interest soon increases. The coach may occasionally refer to them ("Remember that the evidence Q&As are here for your use if you think they'll help you") but no explicit instruction to use them is given. Suggested Q&A sets for a number of topics appear in the appendix.

Figure 3-2 illustrates a few questions from an evidence set for the abortion topic. The question is printed on the outside and the question with its answer is on the inside of the folded sheet.

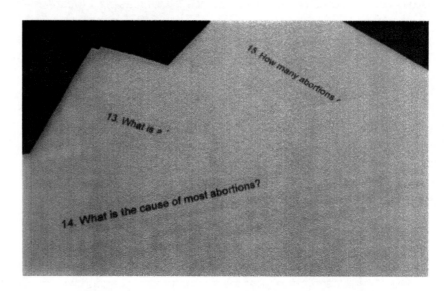

Figure 3-2. Illustration of Q&A Set for Abortion Topic

By year 2, students are ready for evidence to begin to play a more explicit role. An initial evidence set for the topic is introduced and an activity is initiated that directly involves it. Teams divide into small groups (they can further divide into pairs if desired) with the groups dividing up the team's reason cards that were generated at the initial session. An identical set of evidence Q&As is distributed to each group and the coach asks, "Could the answers to any of these evidence questions help support one of your reasons?" If so, students are instructed to summarize the evidence in a sentence on a sticky note and attach it to the reason card. In subsequent activities, groups review one another's work and make additions and revisions.

AV5 Students generate questions about the China One-Child Policy topic.

We have found that students quickly progress to taking over the role of generating their own evidence questions, which attract more interest and debate than the initial adult-generated questions. We therefore suggest that students be offered this opportunity early on. The ease with which students take on this role has been one of the most startling observations from our experience with this curriculum. The questions bubble up slowly, but then take off, with some classes eventually generating 50 or more questions per topic by the time the topic cycle is completed. (See appendix for examples.)

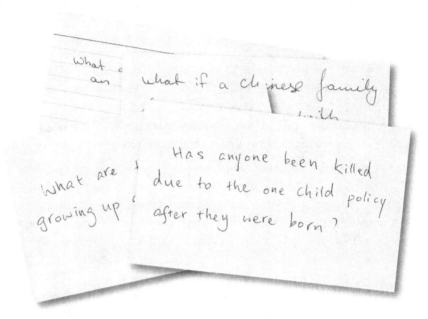

Figure 3-3. Student-Generated Questions for the China One-Child Policy Topic

Coaches provide brief factual answers to student-generated questions by the next class session, sometimes instead returning a question to a student for better formulation. A submitted question that does not allow a simple factual answer (e.g., "Are Chinese children sad they don't have brothers or sisters?") is best returned to the student for rewriting, with suggestions for how it might be developed into one that could be more easily answered.

This "evidence Q&A set" becomes a resource for the entire class, circulated and shared (either with duplicate paper copies or a master list projected or posted where students can easily access it). Toward the end of year 2, we've experimented with having students volunteer to spend a class session or two at an "evidence desk," where they work with an assistant coach using the Internet to seek answers to the questions that classmates have generated.

When students become familiar and comfortable with the activity of attaching evidence to their reasons, the coach can begin to emphasize the multiple relations and directions that connect claims and evidence. Once students begin to debate their opponents, they should begin to recognize the role of evidence in weakening, as well as supporting, more than one reason.

Another change that may occur from year 1 to year 2 is that teams might profit from the addition of a third pre-game session, in which they continue the attaching-evidence activity from session 2. In this case, groups work with different reason cards and/or different pieces of evidence that they have not worked with in session 2, exchanging with other groups and groups again reviewing one another's work. Alternatively, if the available evidence has been largely examined and contemplated by the end of session 2, the class can move on to the next and central phase of the curriculum, the Game Phase.

> 🎥 **AV6 With coaching, students work on connecting reasons and evidence and seeking evidence to fill gaps they identify.**

Optional reading. A question teachers might ask at this point is, "Don't students need to be provided with background knowledge on these complex, unfamiliar topics before they can talk intelligently about them?" This question is its own topic for debate, with pros and cons to each side, and anyone who chooses to work with this curriculum will have to come to his or her own decision. On one hand, additional initial input, in the form of assigned reading, may enable students to generate richer initial arguments. On the other, too much initial input may lead students to look to a source of authority for answers, discouraging them from developing their own ideas and taking seriously those of their peers, thereby feeling greater ownership of the activity.

In the absence of a right-or-wrong answer, the good news is that the curriculum can work well either way—with or without supplemental reading that students are assigned to do in class or as assignments to be completed outside of class. As a resource for teachers, we have included in the appendix for a number of topics a sampling of brief passages that can be used for this purpose. These, note, are well balanced, either within the passage or by means of side-by-side passages written from opposing perspectives.

Taking Stock

Whether it occupies two sessions or three, it is useful for the Pre-Game Phase for both years 1 and 2 to conclude with a final assessment and evaluation of where each team stands—an activity students can be encouraged to conduct on their own albeit briefly. Are their reasons organized into better and best ones and are they ready to face the opposition? Especially in the initial year 1 cycles, some drama can be invoked at this point, reminding novice arguers that while they have been doing their hard work, the other side has been doing the same thing. At the next class, their arguments will be revealed, and they are going to have to be paid attention to.

Game Phase: Confronting and Addressing Opposing Views (Sessions 3–8)

Overview: What happens in the Game phase?

- Students assemble into pairs within pro and con teams.
- Each pair engages in an electronic dialog with a pair from the opposing side.
- At each session, a new opposing pair is encountered.
- Students reflect on their dialogs and continue to generate new evidence to support and critique arguments.

Game Phase: Links to Key Competencies from Common Core State Standards

- Use technology, including the Internet, to produce and publish writing and present the relationships between information and ideas efficiently as well as to interact and collaborate with others. [W.8.6]

- Pose and respond to specific questions with elaboration and detail by making comments that contribute to the topic, text, or issue under discussion. [SL. 6.1c]

Game Phase: Links to Key Competencies from Next Generation Science Standards

- Construct and present oral and written arguments supported by empirical evidence and scientific reasoning to support or refute an explanation or a model for a phenomenon or a solution to a problem. [MS-PS2-4]

The Game phase constitutes the core of the sequence. Students now encounter peers who have similarly spent time contemplating the topic but have taken a position that opposes theirs. During the Pre-Game phase students' ideas will largely have met with acceptance from like-minded peers. This will no longer be the case.

Collaborating with a Same-Side Peer

In this phase, students will work with another student from their team as a same-side pair. This pair debates the topic with a succession of pairs from the opposing side. Working with a same-side partner gives students added confidence they may need. They are not facing the opponent alone. In informal verbal exchange, they develop and try out their ideas with their same-side peer before these are communicated electronically to the opposing pair. Cognitively, the advantage is that thinking that otherwise would be locked within individual minds gets externalized. Once it is expressed it becomes an object of reflection that same-side peers can contemplate: "Is this the best thing to say to them? The best way to answer their criticism?" Thinking develops as a result.

If students do not have prior experience doing collaborative work with peers, coaches will need to emphasize the need to do so, especially at first, and then reiterate as needed. One member of the pair typically types the communication to the opponents (this can rotate). But coaches should emphasize that nothing should be typed until the pair has discussed and agreed upon what is going to be said. This instruction will likely need to be reiterated, initially until students get used to the practice, but also later on, when they may be tempted to cut corners by dividing the workload ("You do this one, I'll do the next.").

AV7 Same-side pairs collaborate in deciding what to say to their opponents.

Teachers will likely draw on their own experience and preferences in constructing the same-side pairs to work together during the Game phase. One practice we have found useful is to pair a student who has been on team A during the previous phase with a student who has been on team B, since they will likely bring somewhat different thinking from their same-side team work. Beyond that, there are no hard-and-fast rules. We have found same-gender pairs more productive at the middle-school level. We have also found it most productive to pair less able students with partners of similar ability level, so that both have the opportunity to feel empowered and to develop their skills, rather than have a high-ability or highly verbal student take over the action, leaving the lesser-ability student at the risk of becoming only an observer. Some teachers, however, may prefer to form mixed pairs.

Communicating with Opponent Pairs

The hardware and software used for this phase will vary greatly according to circumstances, and hence we comment here only in general terms. Many different kinds of chat applications are available, but we have found the simplest ones work quite adequately. We have found Google to be extremely easy to set up and use for this purpose. The available tools include Google Talk (known informally as gchat) and Google Drive, which houses Google Docs. Netbooks work as well as conventional laptops as hardware. If software and/or hardware aren't available, even the Pass-the-Pad method (see Chapter 5) can suffice. Whatever the tools used, the teacher or head coach will want to prepare a rotation schedule like the one shown in Figure 3-4.

Once each same-side pair is connected to its opponent pair, the electronic discourse begins. If there is a brief delay as the electronic connections get established, students can be encouraged to discuss with their partner what arguments they anticipate hearing from their opponents and how they might be able to respond. Once everyone is ready to begin, either the pro or the con pairs are designated to begin with an opening communication to their opposing pair. As illustrated in Chapter 5, dialogs initially are likely to reflect a preoccupation with mechanics, but this soon changes. Students are instructed they should try to convince opponents that their own position is the stronger one. As we noted in Chapter 2, students initially may not attend closely or at all to what their opponents say, carrying on with their own argument when it is their turn. Once students are comfortable with the method, coaches can begin gentle reminders to attend to what their opponents say and address it. Even if they think the opponents' claims are weaker than their own, students should be reminded, they should not be ignored.

Chat 1: March 27	Pro goes 1st (TYPE YOUR NAMES!)	P1 vs C1	P2 vs C2	P3 vs C3	P4 vs C4	P5 vs C5	P6 vs C6	P7 vs C7	P8 vs C8
Chat 2: March 29	Con goes 1st (TYPE YOUR NAMES!)	P1 vs C2	P2 vs C3	P3 vs C4	P4 vs C5	P5 vs C6	P6 vs C7	P7 vs C8	P8 vs C1
Chat 3: April 3	Pro goes 1st (TYPE YOUR NAMES!)	P1 vs C3	P2 vs C4	P3 vs C5	P4 vs C6	P5 vs C7	P6 vs C8	P7 vs C1	P8 vs C2
Chat 4: April 5	Con goes 1st (TYPE YOUR NAMES!)	P1 vs C4	P2 vs C5	P3 vs C6	P4 vs C7	P5 vs C8	P6 vs C1	P7 vs C2	P8 vs C3
Chat 5: April 17	Pro goes 1st (TYPE YOUR NAMES!)	P1 vs C5	P2 vs C6	P3 vs C7	P4 vs C8	P5 vs C1	P6 vs C2	P7 vs C3	P8 vs C4
Chat 6: April 19	Con goes 1st (TYPE YOUR NAMES!)	P1 vs C6	P2 vs C7	P3 vs C8	P4 vs C1	P5 vs C2	P6 vs C3	P7 vs C4	P8 vs C5

Figure 3-4. Sample Dialog Rotation Schedule

At the next session, the activity is repeated with new opponents and the dialog sessions continue until all pairs have debated all opposing pairs. (In the case of a very small group, repeat encounters can occur, to afford students sufficient practice within the Game phase.)

Reflecting

What does a pair do while waiting for the opposing pair to respond? There are a number of possibilities, but the one we have found most effective is to have them proceed to the reflection component of the curriculum. The whole curriculum has reflection as its objective, but some components are explicitly reflective. The most explicit of these are the reflection sheets that become a regular part of the dialog sessions. These are printed sheets that students complete in pen or pencil. Students are able to work on them while awaiting their opponents' responses. Only one reflection sheet is distributed to a pair at a given session, and students are instructed to collaborate on it, as they do in the dialogs themselves. They are collected and saved at the end of the session, as they will be used again.

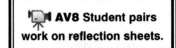
AV8 Student pairs work on reflection sheets.

Reflection sheets are of two types, best alternated across sessions. Each of the two types appears following the year 1 and year 2 curriculum guides in the appendix. Questions from the "Other" sheet are: "What is one of their main arguments and what was our response (counterargument)? Was there a better counterargument to use?" Questions from the "Own" sheet are: "What is one of our main arguments and what was their counterargument and our comeback (rebuttal)? Was there a better Comeback we could have used?"

Because students have the accumulated record of the dialog sitting in front of them on their computer screens, they are able to review and reflect on it as the basis for answering these questions. Hence, they don't begin work on it until some dialog has accumulated. Prior to this, they can use waiting time to discuss with their partner how they think their opponents will respond and how they might be able to respond in turn. If a more structured activity is needed, pairs can be given a sheet on which to predict what their opponents will say and then to score themselves on whether they were correct.

Figure 3-5. Sample Completed Other-Side Reflection Sheet

During year 2, students will be working explicitly with evidence. This can be added to the reflection sheet in the form of a sticky note that summarizes the evidence and is affixed to the appropriate argument, counterargument, or rebuttal. The coach may comment, "A reflection sheet isn't really finished until it has some evidence on it." Also, throughout this phase, coaches remind students to use the cards provided to ask new questions that may occur to them that they would like answers to.

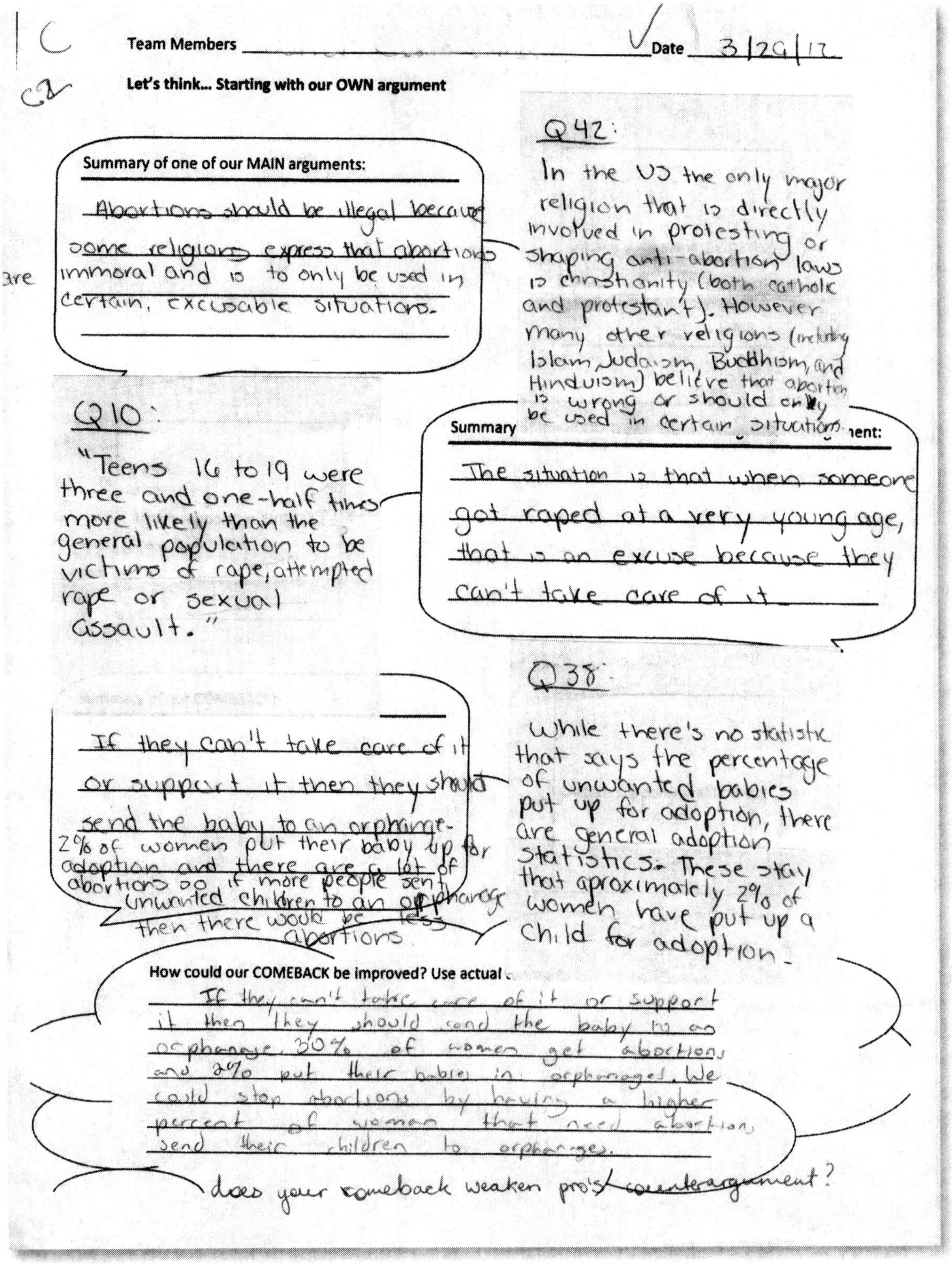
C

C2

Team Members ____ Date 3/29/12

Let's think... Starting with our OWN argument

Summary of one of our MAIN arguments:

Abortions should be illegal because some religions express that abortions are immoral and is to only be used in certain, excusable situations.

Q42: In the US the only major religion that is directly involved in protesting or shaping anti-abortion laws is christianity (both catholic and protestant). However many other religions (including Islam, Judaism, Budhism, and Hinduism) believe that abortion is wrong or should only be used in certain situations.

Q10: "Teens 16 to 19 were three and one-half times more likely than the general population to be victims of rape, attempted rape or sexual assault."

Summary ... ment:

The situation is that when someone got raped at a very young age, that is an excuse because they can't take care of it

Q38: While there's no statistic that says the percentage of unwanted babies put up for adoption, there are general adoption statistics. These stay that aproximately 2% of women have put up a child for adoption.

If they can't take care of it or support it then they should send the baby to an orphange. 2% of women put their baby up for adoption and there are a lot of abortions so if more people sent unwanted children to an orpharage then there would be less abortions.

How could our COMEBACK be improved? Use actual ...

If they can't take care of it or support it then they should send the baby to an orphanage. 30% of women get abortions and 2% put their babies in orphanages. We could stop abortions by having a higher percent of women that need abortion, send their children to orphanges.

does your comeback weaken pro's ~~counterargument~~?

Figure 3-6. Sample Completed Own-Side Reflection Sheet with Evidence Attached

During year 2, students may tire of the reflection sheets and be ready for a different reflective activity. In this case, either as homework or an in-class activity, they can be assigned a dialog excerpt, either of their own or of another (anonymous) pair, and asked to evaluate each contribution to the dialog with respect to how well it addresses and weakens the previous statement in the dialog. (See Chapter 6 for an illustration of this and another more advanced reflective activity.)

End-Game Phase (Sessions 9–13)

The End-Game phase moves into the preparation for and culmination of the sequence in students' eyes, the Showdown (session 11) in which the two sides come together in a final whole-class debate. First, students are told, they must return to their same-side teams to confer and make sure they are ready for the Showdown. Session 9 is devoted to review of the other side's position, and how they will counter it. Session 10 is devoted to their own side, how the opponents are likely to challenge it, and how they can address these challenges.

End-Game Phase: Links to Key Competencies from Common Core State Standards

- Delineate a speaker's argument and specific claims, evaluating the soundness of the reasoning and relevance and sufficiency of the evidence and identifying when irrelevant evidence is introduced. [SL.8.3]

- Respond thoughtfully to diverse perspectives; synthesize comments, claims, and evidence made on all sides of an issue; resolve contradictions when possible; and determine what additional information or research is required to deepen the investigation or complete the task. [SL.11-12.1d]

End-Game Phase: Links to Key Competencies from Next Generation Science Standards

- Evaluate the claims, evidence, and reasoning behind currently accepted explanations or solutions to determine the merits of arguments. [HS-LS2-6]

- Evaluate the evidence behind currently accepted explanations or solutions to determine the merits of arguments. [HS-LS2-8]

Reviewing Opponents' Arguments (Session 9)

By now students will have had a great deal of experience in encountering opponents' arguments in the dialogs they have had with them and in developing their skills in countering those arguments. Their first task now is to review those arguments.

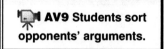

AV9 Students sort opponents' arguments.

Organizing opponents' arguments. To accomplish this task, students reassemble in their same-side teams and the set of other-side reflection sheets that students produced during their dialogs is returned to them. (These, recall, begin with "One of the other side's main arguments was. . . .") The sheets are divided arbitrarily among the small groups within same-side teams and the group's task is to sort them into piles, each pile representing a unique other-side argument. Groups can then join together to integrate their piles and form a final set. At all points, groups have the opportunity to add other-side arguments that they are aware of that are not represented in

AV10 Students sort opponents' arguments and identify strongest ways to counter them.

the reflection sheets. All of this work is valuable in demanding close reflection on the opposing arguments.

Countering opponents' arguments. The task is now to identify the best one or two counterarguments that can weaken each of the opponents' arguments. For this purpose students review counterarguments and complete a colored summary sheet to affix to each reason pile, indicating what these best counterarguments are. Students are reminded these will be very helpful when they are needed quickly during the Showdown.

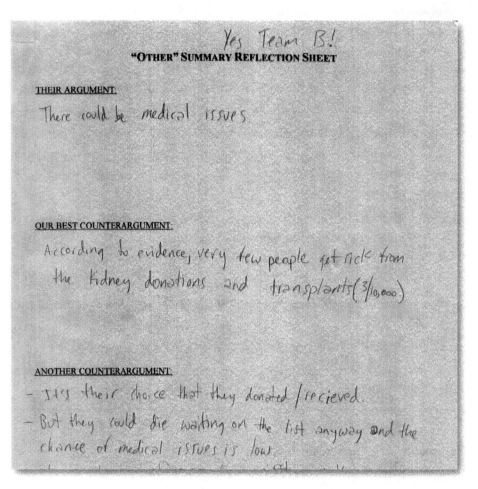

Figure 3-7. Sample Other-Side Summary Reflection Sheet

Reviewing Own Arguments (Session 10)

Organizing one's own arguments. The objective of this session is to apply the same scrutiny to the students' own arguments. Similar to the preceding session, this session begins with sorting the set of reflection sheets into piles, each representing a unique reason, but this time the procedure is applied to own-side reflection sheets. Again, at all points, groups have the opportunity to add own-side arguments that they are aware of that are not represented in the reflection sheets.

AV11 Students sort own arguments and identify strongest ways to rebut opponents' counterarguments.

Identifying counters to own arguments and rebuttals. Students are again given a (differently) colored summary sheet to affix to each own-argument pile. This time, however, there are two more steps to complete. First they must review the reflection sheets to identify the strongest, most damaging one or two counters to this argument and these are noted on the colored summary sheet for each unique argument. Then, most demanding, using the existing reflection sheets as a resource, they need to decide on the strongest way to rebut this counterargument, in order to save their own argument, and these rebuttals (or "comebacks") are recorded on the summary sheet, to be ready for use during the Showdown.

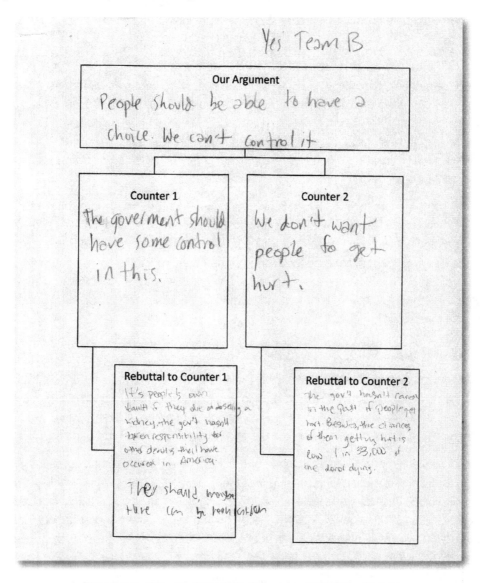

Figure 3-8. Sample Own-Side Summary Reflection Sheet

Showdown (Session 11)

The Showdown session is the most exciting one for students and what they see as the culmination of all their preparation to this point. The class will observe as one student after another comes to the front of the class (the "hot seat") to verbally debate a classmate from the opposing side. One of the sides will be declared a winner at the end of Session 12. From the adult perspective the demanding cognitive work that students do before and after the Showdown is the purpose of the time that has been invested and a worthy end in itself.

From this perspective, the Showdown itself is expendable. Coaches should nonetheless support students in embracing the drama of this occasion.

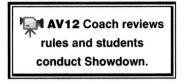

There is no single right way to conduct the Showdown, allowing considerable flexibility to adjust to particular circumstances. The appendix curriculum guides and the video clip identify procedures we have found useful. Whatever specific rules are adopted, for the first few topic sequences students will need to be introduced to them and review them. This can be done at the end of the preceding session, if time permits, or at the beginning of the Showdown session.

Each side should assemble on opposite sides of the room; depending on group size, half the students can be the "on duty" active teams, switching roles with the "advisory" teams (who can send notes to the active team) midway through. Each side should have access to all their own earlier generated materials, but students in the two "hot seats" do not bring materials or notes with them. Instead, a procedure we have found very productive is to allow either hot-seat speaker or their respective active teams to call a "huddle" whenever desired, to confer with the speaker from their side. Following the huddle, speakers return to their hot seats, presumably armed with some new ideas.

Teams will vary, and vary across time, in how much adult guidance they need to organize themselves into a sequence of team members who will take turns in the hot seat. Some groups will be able to do this unassisted; coaches may need to assist other groups, making sure the role rotates fairly and in particular encouraging individual students who may feel timid about taking on the role. Time limits for turns in the hot seat and for huddles should be decided in advance (we have found 2 minutes and 1 minute about right for each) and then strictly enforced. The next occupant of the hot seat should be reminded to pick up where the previous occupant left off, rather than start the discussion anew.

Showdown Debrief (Session 12)

The debrief session ideally is the most intellectually productive session of the sequence. Students' interest is engaged and they are prompted to reflect on their own and their peers' thinking and evaluate it. During the first topic or two, students will be interested to see a video recording of part of the Showdown, but after a few topic sequences their interest will be focused more on the analysis and scoring of the debate.

Coaches will have selected portions of the Showdown discourse to transcribe and present to the class as an argument map (one side's statements appearing in the left column and the other side's in the right) for analysis, with points indicated for strong and weak moves. Scoring criteria and debrief discussion can be employed flexibly to match students' ability level. A central focus should be positive scoring of counterargument (and rebuttal), with use of evidence (and avoidance of unwarranted assumptions) receiving greater emphasis in year 2. (See appendix examples.)

A winning team is announced at the end of the session, based on the scoring of the showdown transcript or recording prior to the session. Teachers adopting the curriculum may feel uneasy about their role in eval-

uating and assigning scores to the individual moves students make in the Showdown. They should be reassured, however, that there is no absolute "right or wrong" score to be applied. Instead, the feedback students receive at the debrief should be geared to their own levels of understanding of argumentive discourse, which we of course hope will be developing as they participate in the curriculum. Hence, we have found that scoring can become more demanding over time. Initially, the scoring will rest to a large degree on whether or not students respond to one another, addressing their opponents' points, with standards regarding the quality of a counterargument less demanding. Later, attempted but unsuccessful counterarguments can be distinguished from successful ones, with only the latter receiving a positive score.

As a resource, we have included two kinds of illustrations of scoring and debrief. One is a video of most of an entire debrief session presented to a class completing their first year of the curriculum. A reader may want to view it in its entirety or view just a bit of it to get the idea. The second resource, in the appendix, is a sample of Showdown exchanges with suggested scoring.

Essay Preparation and Final Essay (Session 13)

A key component of the sequence is the final essay students write once all other activities have been completed. This is the true culminating event in the sequence, even though students are more likely to see the Showdown as culmination. Here students have the opportunity to interiorize all the dialogic thinking about the topic that has occurred to this point and to express it in more conventional written form.

Culminating Essay: Links to Key Competencies from Common Core State Standards

- Introduce precise, knowledgeable claim(s), establish the significance of the claim(s), distinguish the claim(s) from alternate or opposing claims, and create an organization that logically sequences claim(s), counterclaims, reasons, and evidence. [W.11-12.1a.]

- Provide a concluding statement or section that follows from the argument presented. [W.6.1e.]

To prepare the way for this transition from dialogic to interior and individual, an intervening "Pre-Write" activity can take place during this final session, before students write their final essays. (See appendix supplementary material.) Essays can be written in class or as a homework assignment.

Final essays can be written in the form of a newspaper Op-ed or Letter to the Editor. The box on the next page contains a guideline students can be given for the assignment.

Essays should be completed and submitted by the next session, when a new topic sequence begins. In the next chapter, we look closely at how students' essays develop as they repeat with new topics the sequence described in this chapter.

Student Guideline for "Letter to the Editor" Topic Essay

You have now thought deeply about a topic for 6 weeks and debated your ideas with classmates. Now it's time for you to take your own stand on this issue and to communicate it clearly and persuasively. Think of the newspaper reader who will read your letter, and who may be undecided about the issue. Get your message across to that reader.

The thinking:

Have you communicated strong, clear reasons in favor of your position? What is your evidence? Could someone argue against these reasons? Anticipate what they could say and include a response to it.

Have you addressed the other side's position? What arguments/reasons support their position? What evidence do they have? Can you challenge their position? Are their arguments as strong as yours? If not, why not?

Have you connected your points into an overall argument in which you weigh both sides and take a final position?

The writing:

Make it short but rich. Letters to the Editor cannot be long. Yours should be a maximum of 300 words. You may want to write more at first, then work at eliminating extra words and getting what you have to say into the fewest words you can, without losing any of your meaning.

Have you communicated clearly to your reader? Is each sentence written clearly enough to make sense to the reader? Does each sentence connect to both the previous one and the next one, to make a meaningful paragraph?

The format:

Maximum length 300 words. Use the model of a Letter to the Editor. Remember to include the date, the salutation (Dear Editor:), and your signature, and print your name and the name of your school clearly.

LIST OF VIDEO CLIPS

AV1. Coaches give opening instructions 0:37 seconds
AV2. Coaches give instructions for sharing reasons 1:40 seconds
AV3. Students sharing reasons 1:15 seconds
AV4. Students evaluate and categorize reasons 0:27 seconds
AV5. Students generate questions about topic 0:35 seconds
AV6. Connecting reasons and evidence and seeking evidence to fill gaps 3:30 seconds
AV7. Same-side pairs collaborate in deciding what to say to their opponents 1:35 seconds
AV8. Student pairs work on reflection sheets 0:57 seconds
AV9. Students sort opponents' arguments 2:32 seconds
AV10. Students sort opponents' arguments and identify strongest ways to counter them 1:24 seconds
AV11. Students sort own arguments and identify strongest ways to rebut opponents' counterarguments 1:46 seconds
AV12. Coach reviews rules and students conduct showdown 7:24 seconds
AV13. Showdown debrief 31:13 seconds

Chapter 4

■ ■ ■

Developing Argumentive Writing

I N THIS CHAPTER, WE ILLUSTRATE THE GAINS STUDENTS SHOW in individual expository writing over the course of their participation in our curriculum. The potential of this curriculum to enhance students' nonfiction expository writing is likely the aspect of greatest interest to middle-school and high-school teachers reading this book. In contemplating using the curriculum, teachers will want to know most of all what it will do for their students' writing. Hence, as we now go on to examine students' cognitive growth during the course of their participation in the curriculum we have described, we first portray developments in individual writing. This portrayal, we hope, will serve as a roadmap for teachers that can inform their own work in developing these skills in their students—here are milestones to look for. In the next chapter we identify corresponding changes we have observed in students' dialogic argumentation over the course of the curriculum.

Links to Key Competencies from Common Core State Standards

Write arguments to support claims with clear reasons and relevant evidence. [W.6.1]

Links to Key Competencies from Next Generation Science Standards

Construct and present oral and written arguments supported by empirical evidence and scientific reasoning to support or refute an explanation or a model for a phenomenon or a solution to a problem. [MS-PS2-4]

Giving Writing a Purpose

We have emphasized the core idea that rich engagement in discourse serves as a scaffold to support development in individual written (or individual verbal) argument. As beginning writers, students need to see a clear purpose to their writing, beyond merely trying to produce "what the teacher wants." As we noted in Chapter 1, too often students fail to see the point of an expository writing assignment. Lacking a dialogic structure, they seek to string together a series of statements they think no one would take objection to, and the result is flat and without purpose. Dialog provides the "missing interlocutor" that gives written argument a point.[1] Students can now identify the recipients of their communication, and they have a clear purpose for communicating. Anticipating the recipients' response is a powerful tool that energizes and shapes their communication.

The interlocutor and purpose provided by discourse thus serve as a foundation for argumentive writing. Discourse as a scaffold for such writing is the core of what our curriculum provides. Experiencing a real interlocutor and a purpose to the dialogs they engage in with their classmates enables students to interiorize this dialogic frame when it comes time for them to express their own thinking individually in writing. In sitting down to write, students are no longer writing to the teacher, seeking to meet his or her expectations. Instead, they engage with peer interlocutors—first electronically and for real and later confined to their own imaginations, envisioning what this peer might say and how they can address it and anticipating how the peer will respond to what they say.

Thinking as the Foundation for Writing

Beyond its foundation in dialog, the characteristic of our approach that most strongly differentiates it from many others in developing student writing is its central focus on the thinking underlying the writing. What ideas does the writer seek to express and what function does each of these ideas serve in relation to the writer's overall purpose? It is this thinking that we are most interested to see develop, with the writing a manifestation of it. Our curriculum seeks to develop in students the skills and the disposition to think deeply and incisively about complex issues. It is this progress that we examine in this chapter, as it is reflected in students' argumentive writing.

Of course students need to be able to express their thinking in writing—not an easy task, but an essential one, since even the most profound thinking will go unappreciated if it is not well communicated. Even the surface characteristics of writing are not to be ignored. They are essential to effective communication. But they should not become the primary focus, as they too often do in teaching writing. It is the thinking that underlies what one writes that must be firmly in place if the writing is to be worth reading.

Does our approach succeed in developing the thinking that underlies students' argumentive writing? If so, what kinds of changes can be observed? To address these questions, in this chapter we examine samples of writing that 6th- and 7th-grade students produced while participating in our curriculum. We focus on the individual essays that students are assigned to write at the end of each topic cycle, after they have engaged with the topic in depth and debated it with their peers in varying formats over seven weeks. This is a student's final "position paper" on the topic—a chance to express where they now stand with respect to the topic and why, in the form of a newspaper Op-ed or Letter to the Editor conveying their position on the issue.

The students whose work we present in this chapter are ethnically diverse middle-school students at an urban public middle school (see Chapter 6 for details). They are students from several classes at the same middle school as students whose work appears in Chapter 3. Over a period of five years, a number of classes participated in the curriculum twice weekly for at least two years, during which time they typically wrote seven final essays as the culminating activity in their engagement with each of seven different topics. In this chapter we examine their essays on the first topic, written near the beginning of 6th grade, and the last topic, written near the end of 7th grade.

In the absence of any special curriculum, we would expect to see at least the surface aspects of students' writing improve with practice during the critical middle-school years as their overall literacy grows, and this was the case as reflected in school-based assessments. In their ELA classes, they were taught the standard five-paragraph essay framework and they had more assigned writing practice than is typical in most public middle schools. As reflected in the essays excerpted here, students learned to use a spell-checking program efficiently, making their essays easier to read. Our goal here is to go beyond these aspects to look for development in the argumentive thinking that underlies their writing.

In Chapter 6, we provide a quantitative summary of the progress we trace in this chapter. Also, briefly in this chapter and again in Chapter 6, we report on what constitutes a crucial test of the curriculum – students' writing on a new topic they had not encountered as part of the curriculum. We did not expect (and did not find) essays on new, unfamiliar topics to be of the same quality as students' final topic essays within the curriculum. In the latter case students have been engaged with the topic for 13 class sessions and participated in a highly motivating Showdown debate and debrief. They have thought a lot about the topic and contemplated a wide range of ideas and evidence related to it. Yet comparison of essays on a new topic with essays written as part of the curriculum addresses a critical question: Are any gains they show confined to contexts in which students have devoted substantial time and cognitive and emotional investment in the topic?

This is a critical question, as the academic essay writing required of students rarely has these characteristics. To address the question in a rigorous way, we ask all students who have participated in our curriculum to complete an in-class essay assignment, at the beginning and again at the end of each year of their participation, on a topic not included in the curriculum. (The topic we have used most often is whether teachers' pay should be equal or experience-based.) We assess the extent to which the final essay reflects cognitive gains, both compared to the student's own earlier essay and compared to essays of a matched control group who have not participated in the curriculum. In short, and elaborated in Chapter 6, the gains students show on these essays establish that their progress is more general than the changes they show on the particular curriculum topics we examine in this chapter. We turn now to what these changes look like.

How Does Argumentive Writing Grow?

The key development in argumentive thinking that we looked for first in student essays parallels the one we look for in their dialogic argument with their peers. Does the writer go beyond making a case for the favored position to acknowledge and attempt to address the opposing position and arguments? As we noted in Chapter 1, genuine arguments are those situated in a framework of alternatives. If there are no alternatives, no argument need be made. It is this attention to alternatives that we hope students will develop through dialog.

Once this dialogic focus is achieved, will it transfer to the context of individual written argument? No longer is an opposing position personified in a flesh-and-blood other who expresses and elaborates it, thereby providing a ready object to address. As effective writers we must be able to generate that opposing position ourselves and to know that we should do so. We must then hold it to the light for our own inspection. Along with examining and addressing the opposing position, we need to develop the case in favor of our own position, making effective use of arguments and evidence that can be brought to bear in support of it, but also, and equally critical, anticipating opponents' counterarguments and contemplating how they can best be addressed. And doing so entails taking into account the relevant evidence that bears not just on one's own but also on the opponent's position. In a word, the cognitive demands of argumentive writing are formidable.

To what extent do students who participate in our argument curriculum become capable of meeting these challenges? Students do not all of a sudden become deep thinkers. The gains they make are largely slow and incremental, and their initial achievements are not high-level ones, particularly among students who have had little previous practice in expressing ideas in writing or even in expressing them at all. The initial achievements we trace here, however, are the cognitive building blocks that lay the way for students' further development as thinkers and writers.

What Does an Argument Accomplish?

Our goal is thus to look for deep structural changes over time in students' essays, ones that reflect growing command of argumentive thinking. Toward this end we identified the individual idea units contained in each of the first (written near the beginning of 6th grade) and last (written near the end of 7th grade) topic essays of students from two classes who participated in the curriculum during these years.

The key question we wanted to ask about each idea was how the idea was used. In other words, what argumentive function did it serve? What does it accomplish that will contribute to the overall argument and move it along? We identified four basic functions, two devoted to "my side" (M) of the argument and two to the opponent's side (O), with each playing either a supporting (+) or critiquing (–) role regarding that position:

Support my position (M+). An idea that serves to support one's own position.

Weaken other's position (O–). An idea that critiques and thereby attempts to weaken the opponent's position.

Support other's position (O+). An idea that acknowledges a strength of the opponent's position.

Weaken my position (M–). An idea that acknowledges a weakness of one's own position.

Thus, for example, the position that parents should be allowed to home school their child (the initial topic for these students), ideas supporting the position would be categorized as M+, while ideas against this position, noting its drawbacks, would be categorized as M–. Ideas in support of the opposing position, that the child should be required to attend the town school, would be categorized as O+, while ideas against the town school position would be categorized as O–.

Which of these four kinds of statements did students use most often in their essays? It is not surprising to learn that Support-own (M+) statements were by far the most prevalent of the four functions, both in students' initial topic essays and in their final topic essays. This did not change over time. All students included many Support-own statements in both initial and final essays. Thus, they sought primarily to support their own position with relevant arguments. This is what most of us do, most of the time, when we argue for something we believe.

Second most frequent were Weaken-other (O–) statements, statements in which the writer identifies and addresses the opposing position and seeks to weaken it by pointing out its deficiencies. Almost all students included such statements in the essays they wrote at the conclusion of the first topic sequence of the curriculum, early in their 6th grade year. This is significant as it tell us that after only one topic sequence—13 class sessions—almost all students had become aware of the need to address the opposing position, precisely what we have claimed is missing in young adolescents' argument and hoped to see develop.

Essays overall didn't get longer over time, influenced perhaps by the reminder students received before each essay of how important it was to be succinct in a newspaper Op-ed submission. (Total number of idea units remained about the same from first to final topic essay—an average of 360 words and 22.2 idea units in the initial essay and 322 words and 20.5 idea units in the final essay.) Over time, the frequency of Weaken-other statements also remained about the same. The number of Support-own statements, however, declined (and as a result the *proportion* of statements devoted to other functions increased).

What replaced the declining proportion of Support-own statements? Changes in the remaining two categories—Support other (O+) and Weaken own (M–) are possibilities. Use of Weaken own, however, remained negligible over time, used by less than a third of students even once. Thus, students rarely saw it as appropriate to note weaknesses in their own positions, even though such weaknesses had been pointed out to them abundantly in the dialogs with their opponents.

The story is different, however, for Support-other (O+) statements. These were similarly negligible in initial essays (made even once by only 21 percent of students). In their final topic essays, however, every one of the students in our sample made a Support-other statement at least once, and the average number of such statements increased significantly (from less than one to over four). In sum, then, we see that both kinds of attention to the other's position—Weaken other and Support other—increase over time, but sequentially. Weaken-other statements become prevalent very quickly (with the first topic), while Support-other statements emerge more slowly but eventually achieve the same level of frequency as Weaken-other ones (an average of between four and five per essay).

The slower emergence of Support-other statements, compared to Weaken-other ones, is perhaps not surprising, since the two pose quite different cognitive demands. Weaken other is an argumentive strategy entirely compatible and consistent to employ in conjunction with the overall most frequent strategy, Support own. They work together: My position is right (and here's why) and your position is wrong (and here's why).

In contrast, Weaken-other and Support-other statements stand in opposition to one another. They don't lead to the same conclusion. The arguer thus must hold in mind and coordinate two statements that tip the scale in opposing directions. If skilled arguers are to include them both, then, how do they do it? In making a Support-other statement they possibly take a stance of "I see your point; however...," going on to air their Support-own arguments. Do students in fact do something like this?

To answer this question, we looked for what we can call *However* arguments. These consist of two adjacent idea units, most often a Support-other statement followed by a Support-own or a Weaken-other statement.[2] The two adjacent statements thus stand in opposition to one another—they do not support the same conclusion. To be regarded as a However argument, a further requirement is that the writer connects the two statements, typically by a conjunction such as "however," "but," or "although." Not all essays in which two such contrasting statements appear adjacently qualify as However arguments, since the two may not be connected to one another, with the opposition between them never acknowledged. We present examples shortly.

However arguments, we found, are rare initially (an average of less than one per essay) but increase significantly over time to an average of almost three (2.95) per essay. In the initial 6th-grade essay just over a third of students make even one However argument; by the final 7th-grade essay 95 percent do. Thus, we see that after they have begun to attend to the opposing position and make use of Weaken-other statements to discredit it, students gradually begin not only to make Support-other statements but also to attempt to coordinate them with the Weaken-other and Support-own statements they have made earlier—an important milestone.

From Single to Dual Focus

We turn now to illustrations of this progress, in the form of uncorrected student essays from the set we have indicated. At most an occasional missing word or punctuation is added to enhance comprehensibility. Otherwise, we have inserted only the four function codes (M+, O–, O+, and M–) after each idea unit, to show how these are applied. To save space, we omit students' paragraphing (which is very variable; some students use it to a greater extent than others).

The first topic students debated was the home school topic—whether a family newly arrived from Greece who didn't speak English must send their 12-year-old son to the local school or be permitted to home school the boy. The majority of students write the sort of essay we identified as most common at the end of the first topic cycle—a combination of M+ and O– statements. Rather than ignoring the opposing position, as is typical of much beginning argumentive writing, they acknowledge it and make arguments against it (even though, recall, statements supporting their own position are more numerous).

Some students, however, progress more slowly. We thus begin with representative essays of students who show less sign of initial progress. Their essays look more like the essays students write prior to beginning the curriculum, which typically pay no or scant attention to the opposing view. Here is an example:

> [S8] I think Nick should go to town school because he can get more education there [M+1]. When he goes to town school his parents can go to work to make money [M+2]. Half the money if one stays home to teach Nick while the other is at work. If Nick goes to town school he can make a lot of friends there [M+3]. Some person said that he can go outside and make friends. The only problem is that he don't know how to speak English [O–]. In town school there are experienced teachers [M+1]. unlike Nicks parents that are experienced greek teachers. That's why I think Nick should go to town school.

We see three minimally elaborated Support-own reasons in this essay (my-side reasons, labeled M+1, M+2, M+3). (Note that the same or very similar reason stated a second time is given the same number.) In contrast to what is typical of the initial assessment essays written before the curriculum begins, we see a hint of recognition of an opposing position (in the two sentences beginning "Some person said . . ."), but an opposing position isn't actually identified and the statement is made only to assert its incorrectness—a potentially positive attribute of home school (finding friends outside) wouldn't work because Nick lacks English. (The assertion is nonetheless scored O–, Weaken other, since it includes a potential argument against the home school position.)

Another student's initial essay would perhaps be judged overall as a richer, better developed one. Its argumentive structure, however, is arguably even less developed than S8's, as it consists entirely of my-side reasons with no recognition of an opposing view:

> [S14] I think that Nick should go to town school to make new friends [M+1], support his family and get a good job when he's older [M+2], and so Nick could learn new things [M+3], and learn at the standard level [M+4]. These are the reasons nick should go to town school. Nick should go to townschool to make new friends [M+1]. Town school will give nick a chance to socialize with other children [M+1]. Nick should also go so that he can learn English and be able to talk with other children so that he can communicate better [M+5].

S14's essay continues with another 10 idea units—he is a fluent writer. However, these include no new ideas; each of the 10 repeats one of the five initial ones shown above.

In contrast to S8 and S14, most students' essays at the end of topic 1 achieve what we call a *dual-focus* structure—one consisting of some combination of Support-own and Weaken-other statements. The essay thus succeeds in identifying the opposing positions and marshaling reasons in favor of one and against the other. Here is an example of one such well-developed essay:

> [S30] I think that Nick should be home schooled because his parents feel more comfortable with him being at home [M+1]. Nick doesn't speak English and it will be hard for him to learn a new language without understanding anything [O–1]. He will have to go back to

kindergarten to learn everything that he doesn't know in English [O–2]. He won't be able to interact with kids his age [O–3]. and he will feel lonely without any friends [O–4]. His parents are certified teachers and can provide him with everything that he needs [M+2]. He can interact with kids his age while playing soccer [M+3]. He could study in English and later, make a company for all Greek speakers [M+4]. If Nick doesn't want to go to town school than he shouldn't be forced [O–5]. If Nick has to do homework in English, he will probably have a hard time and won't understand the assignment [O–6]. The town should allow Nick to stay at home because it should be freedom of choice [M+5]. If Nick was a good student, he can continue to be one, just at home [M+6]. His parents know what is best for him [M+7]. and they should make the decision with him [M+8]. If Nick does go to town school, then he will most likely lose his ties to Greece [O–7] and will stop speaking the language because of the work load he has to take care of to catch up to the other kids [O–8]. The other kids will probably make fun of Nick because he doesn't know English [O–9]. and he will be lonely [O–4]. If the town does make Nick go to town school like all the other families, they won't realize that it would be harder for him to go to town school than anyone else because he speaks a totally different language and will not understand anything [O–1]. because no one can tell him what is going on [O–10]. There probably isn't a Greek speaking teacher in the school and the teachers will have a hard time trying to explain to him what the class is learning [O–10]. Nick will not have any way of communicating to kids [O–11]. and he will probably fail his courses if his teachers don't take into consideration that he has no idea how to speak English [O–12]. Nick's life will be miserable with loneliness [O–4]. and hard work [O–13].

This essay is rich in reasons that address both sides. Yet note that they all point in the same direction, toward the same conclusion. One position is portrayed as having numerous unqualified virtues and the opposing side numerous unqualified drawbacks. The conclusion they point to is clear. We turn now to essays that go beyond this dualistic framing.

From Dual to Integrative Focus

Essays going beyond the dualistic focus illustrated above we found unlikely to appear before students begin the second year of the curriculum. Typically, the first sign of progress is the appearance of one or two Support-other statements, even if they are only isolated acknowledgements of a positive characteristic of the opposing position.

An example is this excerpt from S5's final essay on the juvenile justice topic (whether teens should be tried in adult or juvenile court) near the end of year 2. His initial argument in favor of juvenile court is that teens' brains are not fully developed (M+1). He then shifts to an argument intended to weaken the opposing position:

> Teens in adult prison don't have access to good adult role models making it more likely that the teen would commit crimes later in life [O-1].

S5 then advances something more notable, an argument supporting the opposing side:

> Some may argue that the government saves money if they don't have to pay for juvenile detentions. Adult prison costs $50,000, while juvenile detention costs $75,000 [O+1]. However, adult prison has no mandatory release date, so the teen could lose their whole life [O-2]. In juvenile detention, the teen is released at the age of 18 [M+2].Therefore, the teen could be forced to waste their entire life in adult prison, whether or not they have changed [O-2].

S5 finishes his essay with a return to his initial supporting argument regarding brain development (M+1). Why does he introduce the argument about cost favoring the opposing side but then leave it alone, rather than addressing it and possibly trying to dispose of it? We do not know for sure whether it does not occur to him to do so or whether he would like to do so but knows no counterargument that could weaken this claim.

Another way in which Support-other statements emerge in essays is their mention solely in the course of seeking to discount them. An example comes from the final essay of S8 (whose initial essay we saw earlier shows hints of this strategy):

> **[S8] I think that teens who committed crimes should be held in juvenile court because it is less harsh than adult court [M+1]. Adult jail may make the teen stay for 1 year or for life [O–1]. It depends on the crime they made, but in juvenile detention center teens may only stay there till they're 18 years old [M+1]. At age 11-12 children are tried as adults in that age. So the maximum year for a teen to stay in juvenile detention would be 6-7 years [M+1]. In adult jail teens would be there for more than 6-7 years [O–1]. Both adult jail [O–2]. and juvenile detention [M–1]. has violence, but juvenile can prevent it happening [M+2]. The Juvenile Detention Center can change the teen's behavior [M+3]. and so changing the teen may make them a better person [M+4]. Sometimes this may not work and make crimes worse. Teens may not be changed at 18 years old when they are let free which means they will still do bad things [M–2]. Later on in their life their prefrontal cortex would be fully developed at age 25 [M+5]. The prefrontal cortex is part of the brain that helps people make the right choice. In adult jail, instead of changing the people's behavior [O–3] they have job training programs [O+1]. If teens went to adult jail and do the job training program, how would teens get a big benefit? [O–4]. It's not like when the teen gets out of jail he/she go and gets a job. After years and years they would forget [O–5]. So that's why I think that teens should go to juvenile court instead of going to adult jail.**

S8's essays have by now become solidly dualistic, comprising claims either to support his own position or to weaken the opponent's position. It is only toward the end of this essay that we see a hint of Support-other thinking—adult jails offer job training. Although we score it as an O+ statement, S8 doesn't really even acknowledge it as a virtue and instead proceeds immediately to portray it negatively. Similarly, earlier in the essay we see a hint of a Weaken-own (M–) statement—his own as well as the alternative options both risk violence. But again, this possible weakness is invoked only for the purpose of discounting it (M+2). Note also in this essay the successful use of evidence drawn from the set students constructed during their work on this topic (see Table 4-1.)

Table 4-1. Questions Generated by One Class for the Juvenile Justice Topic

Q1.	What is the adult justice system?
Q2.	What is the juvenile justice system?
Q3.	What are the punishments for serious crimes in both justice systems?
Q4.	What are other people's opinions about this topic?
Q5.	How does the adult court system work?
Q6.	Is there a difference between the adult court system and the adult justice system?
Q7.	How many people get STDs in adult prison?
Q8.	Why is the adult age 18 years old?
Q9.	Do people get smarter as they get older?
Q10.	Do children end up like their parents? If not, who/what decides how they turn out?
Q11.	Do parents choose where there children get to go to the juvenile center?

Q12.	Which has more violence, adult jail or juvenile?
Q13.	When is the prefrontal cortex (part of brain) fully developed?
Q14.	Do people get physically abused in prison, if so, what is the average age group?
Q15.	Putting a child in prison could have a severe effect on their education, will they be given tutoring or an educational program in prison?
Q16.	How many kids went to juvenile in 2011?
Q17.	How many adults went to adult jail in 2011?
Q18.	How many teenagers get sent to trial each year?
Q19.	What are the conditions of Juvenile (including casualties such as riots, arguments, fist fights, etc,.)?
Q20.	What are the conditions of "adult jail (including casualties such as riots, arguments, fist fights, etc.)?"
Q21.	Is the time spent in juvenile detention shorter than it is in regular prison?
Q22.	Can you bail out of juvenile? (pay to get out)
Q23.	Why are you considered mature at age 18? (Is the brain fully developed or something?)
Q24.	Can a child serving prison time have a negative effect on their later life?
Q25.	In an adult jail about how much people you have in one single jail cell?
Q26.	What is the nutrition value in adult vs juvie jail food?
Q27.	What are some court cases about this topic? What were the outcomes?
Q28.	What exactly is considered a serious crime and what are its punishments in the adult and juvenile court system?
Q29.	If a juvenile was put in the same prison as adults, would they share a cell? Or would they share time eating or outside together?
Q30.	Does being in jail or juvie change your behavior?
Q31.	What is the official age range of a "juvenile"?
Q32.	What is the longest time period someone has stayed in juvenile?
Q33.	What is the percent of people that get mental problems when they come out of jail?
Q34.	Can jail time affect your health in any negative or positive way?
Q35.	What happens if a person murders or severely hurts someone in prison or juvenile jail?
Q36.	What happens if someone dies from a disease in jail?
Q37.	Does the child/teens maturity affect the outcome of the teens verdict?
Q38.	Does the child's age affect how much time he/she spends in jail?
Q39.	Based on the severity of the crime, can luxurious activity or "free time" be restricted or refined in prison?
Q40.	If being bailed out of prison is an option, does the fine increase or decrease based on age? Or does it stay the same, adult or juvenile.
Q41.	How many kids who get out of Juvenile Prison commit crimes again?
Q42.	How many people who get out of Adult Prison commit crimes again?
Q43.	In TV shows there are characters that easily break out of Prison, is it really that easy to break out?
Q44.	If you are tried as a juvenile too many times are you tried as an adult?
Q45.	Is there a limit to how old or how young you have to be to be put in juvenile or adult prison? (i.e. a 93 year-old man or a 4 year-old child.)
Q46.	Is contact with family more or less based on the form of prison?
Q47.	Do kids learn more from other kids or adults?
Q48.	What does convicted mean?
Q49.	If put in adult justice system, will their jail time increase?
Q50.	What percentage of teens listen to their parents?

Q51.	Do some brains develop slower and ineffectively than others?
Q52.	Do you have an advantage if you are mentally disabled? What fits into the category of mentally disabled?
Q53.	Can mental problems serve as an excuse for a teen's behavior, if so does that change the outcome of where they end up?
Q54.	Is the topic we are discussing dealing with the U.S. justice court or from other countries?
Q55.	What is the current law, where do children go if they commit serious crimes?
Q56.	Can a child defend themselves in court?
Q57.	Would the government save money if they didn't have to pay for a juvenile system?
Note:	All but the first two questions are student-generated. By this seventh topic, students were doing so well generating their own questions that it was no longer necessary for us to provide questions. Students were provided brief answers (one to three sentences) to each question.

An essay by S3 similarly includes a Weaken-own statement. After making several Support-own statements regarding the benefits that juvenile centers provide (M+1,2,3), she states:

> However, juvenile detention centers also contain violence and other negative aspects that can affect the juveniles [M–1].

In contrast to the two preceding essays, however, S3's essay does more than subsequently ignore or dismiss this statement that stands to weaken her own position. Instead she undertakes some reconciliation, albeit a very weak one:

> There are both "ups and downs" to being in a juvenile center rather than an adult prison but I think that the juvenile detention center would "fix" their identities and make the juveniles better people [M+4].

"There are both 'ups and downs' " to the juvenile court position is as close as S3 comes to connecting her M+ and M– statements. Later, however, she more specifically and explicitly connects two opposing claims to one another. She first introduces a version of an immature brain argument (M+5) and then critiques it:

> In addition, juvenile brains aren't fully developed and they are more prone to making mistakes than others. Some would say that "they are not thinking straight". They therefore deserve a chance and shouldn't receive too serious of a punishment [M+5]. On the other hand, others would say that if they knew enough to commit the serious crime, then they know right from wrong. They can tell what they did is wrong and that there are going to be consequences [O+1].

S3 thus succeeds in integrating two opposing statements ("On the other hand . . .") into a However argument. She connects the two claims and acknowledges their opposition.

Realizing Integration

There is one more step, however, to be taken, and S3 does not take it. What S3's integration does not do is point to a way to resolving the opposition between the two statements. S3 connects the two, but she does not truly integrate them.

An excerpt from another essay, by S4, in contrast, achieves such an integration:

> **Even though those opposed to my view would say teens in an adult prison can be kept separate from the bad influences there [O+], it's my belief that such teens will be more likely to lead a life of crime because they are surrounded by hardened criminals [O–]. This may give some teens the idea that they don't have a future.**

S4 can now proceed to a concluding argument in favor of juvenile court, which is exactly what she does.

The most highly developed essays achieve this integration across multiple issues, providing a sound, comprehensive basis for a conclusion. Here is an example:

> **[S9] I think that juveniles who commit crimes should be tried in juvenile court because of various reasons. First off, the juveniles will be put in adult jail, meaning that they will be able to interact sometimes with the adults. Evidence shows that 70% of prisoners released from adult prison are rearrested in the span of the next three years. This means that the juveniles will most likely be influenced doing crimes again after they are released from adult prison [O–1], An opposing side might say that the same can go for juvenile prison [M–1], and that there might not really be a difference in the two jails. However this argument is faulty because there is no evidence to support it since juvenile records are sealed away when the child reaches age 13 [M+1]. Some teens may have been influenced to conduct a crime based on a past trauma, they were forced into it, or they were being abused by their parents [M+2]. The prefrontal cortex (responsible for exercising good judgment) will not have fully developed until the age of 25, so the juveniles may not have known better [M+3]. An opposing side may bring an example of someone younger than a teen who knows better [M–2], but it really depends on the background of the child [M+4]. Another argument is that juveniles can be physically abused by adults in jail, and age is not a factor in bully/abuse [O–2]. An opposing side might say that sometimes teens and adults are kept away from each other [O+1] and if age isn't a factor then they will be abused in juvenile prison as well [M–3]. That may be true, but in juvenile jail, the juveniles have a chance to defend themselves since they are dealing with people of their own age [M+5]. In adult jail, the juveniles will have the right to education, so they will not be halting their education at all [O+2]. Although they can have schooling in [adult] jail, evidence shows that the education system in adult jail is very poor [O–3]. An opposing side may argue that it doesn't matter what jail they go to, they will still get a very poor education [M–4], but that isn't true. Evidence shows that juvenile prison has a much better education program [M+6]. Overall, the teens who have committed these crimes should be tried in juvenile court because it works to their benefit, such as education, bad influence, and a shielding from adult abuse, and they should not be ruled under the harsh adult system since they have not fully developed the power to make the right and good decisions.**

This notable essay makes it clear that the writer has engaged deeply with the topic across a wide range of issues bearing on it and coordinated multiple arguments to justify a final position. Each new statement functions as a However to the preceding one. An O– statement is followed by an M– statement opposing it ("An opposing side might say . . ."), and the M– statement in turn is followed by a new M+ statement opposing it ("However this argument is faulty because . . .").

Another notable feature of S9's essay is the incorporation of evidence, a critical aspect of an argumentive essay that we turn to in the next section.

The Use of Evidence in Argument

Although many of the second-year essays are like S9's in showing impressive strengths for middle-school essays, we have examined these essays principally with respect to the presence of core elements—the building blocks of argumentive thinking and writing. Beyond this, we did not see much evidence of students' attention to the overall structure of their essays. Some undertook concluding paragraphs (something they had been taught to do in ELA classes). But beyond this, essays linked each sentence to the preceding one, either in list fashion or, at their most accomplished, in an argument → counterargument → rebuttal sequence. We saw little in the way of hierarchical structure characteristic of sophisticated argumentive writing, in which subarguments are embedded in higher-order ones. Clearly, the students whose work we observed have a long way to go in becoming skilled expository writers. Nonetheless, we have portrayed here the growth we have seen in what are essential building blocks if such development is to occur.

The one such essential building block that we have made scant mention of in this chapter until now is the use of evidence in argument. This feature does show evolution in students' essays, as well as in their dialogs examined in the next chapter, and warrants examination. The questions students generate and the answers associated with them make their way into the topic essays, as we have seen. Final essays incorporate much greater use of evidence to support claims than do beginning essays. This is an unfair comparison to make directly, however, since the amount of evidence students have available increases steadily from the first topic, where the need for evidence is not emphasized, to later ones in which evidence is introduced and ultimately generated by students' own questions (as illustrated in Table 4-1).

Hence, rather than formally comparing evidence use in students' initial and final topic essays within the curriculum, we turn to their performance on an in-class writing assignment on a new topic, after the curriculum had concluded. The topic is whether cigarette sales should be banned. As one means of assessing their use of evidence in their writing, we provided students the sheet shown in Table 4-2, telling them that this background information might be of help to them in writing their essays, but they were not explicitly instructed to use it. This assessment is also of note as it occurred a full year after students had completed the two-year curriculum.

Our findings showed that a full year after the two-year curriculum had been completed, students performed better than a nonparticipating comparison group from the same school in the use of evidence in their essays on the smoking topic. Students also outperformed another group who had completed only a single year of the curriculum.

Although not explicitly instructed or reminded to do so, in these postcurriculum essays students commonly included evidence to support their claims, drawing both on the sheet provided and on their own knowledge. We conclude this chapter with several representative essays.

[S20] Cigarette sales should be banned in the US because cigarettes are not good for people. According to the information "Approximately 46.6 million US adults smoke cigarettes" and "each year, an estimated 443,000 people die prematurely from smoking". I am not very sure with my opinion because there are also some people that can't stop smoking, which is bad for them, but not only the fact that they smoke, but also the fact that they can't stop smoking. There are people that are so addicted to smoking that if they stop smoking they can even die. I am also not very sure with my opinion because how it is said "thousands of farmers in the US make their living from farming tobacco leaves." So if cigarettes are banned the farmers will lose their jobs and they won't have money to survive with. According to the information "An estimated 17 million Americans try to quit smoking each year, and about 8% of them succeed." This make me realize that if people determine their minds to stop smoking, they probably will, even though its really hard from what I heard. So now that I think about it, cigarettes shouldn't be banned.

[S12] Cigarettes should be banned in the United States because they are bad for people's health. The United States is already looking when it comes to health care and cigarettes are making things worse. $96 billion dollars are spent on health care for cigarette related problems. This kind of money can be better spent and should not be spent on people with an illogical addiction. People who smoke are killing themselves and forcing the country to spend money on their health care. Even though the tobacco industry generates $16.5 billion dollars, the money spent in health care for cigarette smokers is much greater than the money made. If cigarettes were banned, we'd save a lot of money, and people would be healthier.

[S31] Cigarette sales shouldn't be banned in the US. First, if cigarettes are banned people will still sell them secretly. Not only that, this is one way to relieve depression, since not everyone goes toward the option of getting help. Out of about 17 million people who try to quit smoking only 8% succeed. Knowing that some people will waste their money creating programs to help, but think of how many people would even consider doing it. Obviously, those who say that it should be banned would use the fact that millions die from smoking and exposure from second hand smoking. In order to counter that, we should make smoking areas for those who smoke, this way, we can keep kids from being exposed to second hand smoke and this will lower the death rate of those who smoke and who are exposed to it.

[S23] Banning cigarette use in the U.S. would increase the black market use of cigarettes. Smoking has become ingrained in our society that outlawing it would lead to the same happenings as when the government tried to outlaw alcohol. The temperance act failed and more people started using alcohol than ever before, why would we think banning cigarettes would be any different. Although cigarettes do cause premature deaths and illnesses they are part of cultures long standing and vital to everyday occurrences. Not only culturally needed but also economically needed, cigarettes provide billions of dollars to help keep the U.S. economy going. With the banning of cigarettes will come the increase in our great recession. From a health perspective, yes cigarettes are a bad thing, but from the culture, economy, historical perspective it would do more harm than good to outlaw cigarette distribution.

At the time students wrote these essays they had almost finished eighth grade. Most are able to write well spontaneously on a novel topic such as this one, although these essays are on average shorter than their topic essays written as part of the curriculum. Also, the topic is not as clearly structured in terms of two opposing alternatives as are the curriculum topics. Nonetheless most (although not all) students wrote two-sided essays that identify and address both alternatives (ban or allow cigarettes). Moreover, almost all incorporated evidence into their essays, from their own knowledge or the list provided. (A summary of quantitative comparisons appears in Chapter 6.)

Table 4-2. Evidence Set for the Cigarette Topic

1.	The nicotine in cigarettes causes fast-acting chemical reactions in your brain that has been shown to relieve anxiety and nervousness.
2.	Each year, an estimated 443,000 people die prematurely from smoking or exposure to secondhand smoke, and another 8.6 million live with a serious illness caused by smoking.
3.	George Harrison, a musician for the Beatles, was a smoker and died of lung cancer at the age of 58.
4.	Approximately 46.6 million U.S. adults smoke cigarettes.
5.	Thousands of farmers in the U.S. make their living from farming tobacco leaves, and the tobacco industry contributes an average of $16.5 billion to the economy in tax revenue each year.
6.	Phillip Morris is one of several tobacco companies currently fighting for their rights in lawsuits to sell their product freely, as well as for the rights of their customers. They are defending "smokers' rights laws" in court, claiming that smokers are currently discriminated against in being hired for jobs and are unable to smoke when and where they choose.
7.	A woman named Helen Faith Reichert currently lives in New York City; she is 108 years old and has been smoking half a pack of cigarettes every day for over 80 years.
8.	As much as $96 billion a year is estimated lost in medical costs and lost worker productivity due to tobacco use.
9.	An estimated 17 million Americans try to quit smoking each year, and about 8% of them succeed.

Unsurprisingly, students show some variation in how skillfully they use evidence. The writer of the first essay above is able to do little more than identify the two alternatives and note evidence that supports each, and in fact he shifts his opinion in the course of writing the essay. The authors of the two middle essays are better able to make use of the conflicting evidence in the However arguments they construct, and they weigh the arguments to reach conclusions. The author of the final essay introduces evidence of her own and does not make explicit reference to the provided evidence, although her essay makes clear she has weighed its implications. Hence, we can conclude that following their participation in our curriculum, students both recognize the need to support arguments with evidence and have developed the skills that enable them to do so when the situation calls for it.

Conclusions

Most of the essays presented in this chapter display a higher level of thinking and writing than that typically achieved by middle-school students. This is especially notable given that these students are from academically disadvantaged backgrounds and received no explicit instruction on the topics they were writing about. Beyond the brief answers they were provided to their own questions on the topics, students had only their collaborative experience with their peers as the basis for their writing on each topic. Although, as we noted, these essays may lack the hierarchical structure characteristic of sophisticated argumentive writing, in which subarguments are embedded in higher-order ones, by the second year the essays generally link each idea to the preceding one, often in an argument → counterargument → rebuttal sequence, and show increasing ability to integrate opposing ideas into an integrative structure. Hence we are seeing significant development in what we claim to be cognitive building blocks of mature argumentive writing.

The mode of evaluating the essays illustrated in this chapter departs considerably from what middle-school teachers are accustomed to in evaluating their students' written work. Very often as teachers we are gratified if students compose a sequence of sentences that are on topic and make some sense and there are not too many surface errors of form or expression. The case we make here is that there is another layer just beneath the surface that warrants our close attention because it is the layer that reflects the thinking that has great capacity for growth and that is the vital underpinning of argumentive writing.

Teachers will not often have the time to assess student writing in the detailed manner we have illustrated here. But that does not mean that they cannot look for what we have looked for—in a word, the nature of the thinking underlying students' writing. Doing so will reward the effort, because it is here that there is much important growth to be seen and to be nurtured. We thus hope that this chapter offers teachers a kind of roadmap of what kinds of development they may observe in their students' expository, and in particular argumentive, writing. A map of where students are headed, and the milestones along the way, is an essential guide if we are to best support their development as thinkers and writers.

Especially significant to us as a milestone on this roadmap is the dialogic argumentive structure reflected in the better developed of the essays we examined. The dialogic structure of their argumentation with peers has clearly made its way into the writers' essays ("Others might say . . ."). It is this continuing experience of dialog with a succession of peers holding an opposing position, we believe, that makes this opposing position and its accompanying arguments clear and vivid, enough so that the student undertaking to write an individual essay on the topic is able to represent them in the essay and address them in more than a surface way. And, perhaps most important, students recognize the importance of doing so.

In sum, the students whose writing we have sampled here appear to be on a trajectory to become solid argumentive thinkers and writers, evident in these essays as long as a year after the curriculum devoted to this objective has been completed. In the final chapter, we consider the broader implications. First, in the next chapter, we examine how the peer dialogs that are the heart of the curriculum evolve over time. Are there parallel changes to be seen and do they illuminate how such developments make their way into the essays we have examined in this chapter?

Notes

1. Graff, G. (2003). *Clueless in academe: How schooling obscures the life of the mind.* New Haven: Yale University Press.

2. In addition to Support other together with Support own or Weaken other, two other such combinations—Weaken own with Weaken other and Weaken own with Support own—are possible and potentially qualify as However arguments, as they also meet the criterion of standing in opposition to one another.

Chapter 5

■ ■ ■

Developing Argumentive Discourse

I N THIS CHAPTER WE ILLUSTRATE STUDENTS' PROGRESS in their discourse with one another, drawing on dialogs from the same student groups whose writing appears in the previous chapter. As we did there, we describe major changes we identified, followed by illustrations. Again, the changes we trace provide a kind of roadmap of what teachers can expect to see in their own students' progress.

Recall that in the case of discourse, the curriculum provides students two distinct kinds of practice. While they engage in electronic discourse with opposing-side classmates, students must talk to their same-side partners to decide jointly what they will say to their opponents, evaluate how the opponents respond, and decide what to say next. Thus, in this chapter, as well as presenting illustrations of students' electronic dialogs as they evolve with practice, we also include some illustrations of the conversations between same-side partners as they manage the discourse with their opponents. In both cases—the talk between same-side partners and between the opposing pairs—we can see parallels to changes we observed in the previous chapter in students' writing. The changes observed in this chapter thus provide insight into how dialogic practice can both lead to and support students' progress in individual writing.

Links to Key Competencies from Common Core State Standards

Initiate and participate effectively in a range of collaborative discussions . . . with diverse partners . . . building on others' ideas and expressing their own clearly and persuasively. [SL.9-10.1]

Respond thoughtfully to diverse perspectives; synthesize comments, claims, and evidence made on all sides of an issue; resolve contradictions when possible; and determine what additional information or research is required. . . . [SL.11-12.1d]

Links to Key Competencies from Next Generation Science Standards

Construct and present oral and written arguments supported by empirical evidence and scientific reasoning to support or refute an explanation or a model. . . . [MS-PS2-4]

The Beginnings of Discourse: Connecting My Talk to Yours

The initial goals of dialog with peers are to get students first to listen and then to respond to one another. Doing so, we have seen, does not come naturally. In arguing with someone who does not share their view, young people (and even many older ones) are prone to focus on saying what they have to say. They may elaborate and convey their ideas more and more forcefully, seeing this as the path to victory. With persistence, they assume, the opponent's ideas will fade away without so much as a hearing, and their own view will prevail.

With time and experience students abandon this strategy—at least as a first-line or exclusive approach—and they begin to listen to one another. In our study of students' dialogs, we closely examine students' reactions to what their opponents have just said. Do they ignore it, continuing with what they had been saying or turning the conversation in a new direction? Or do they acknowledge what the opponent has said and even respond to it in some manner? If so, what form do these responses take?

At its most minimal, such a response may be nothing more than a superficial acknowledgment, "Yes, but ..." or even "Well, you have a point, but . . ." followed by the speaker's returning to his or her own agenda. Compared to superficial acknowledgment, addressing the substance of what an opponent has said is another, more demanding matter. But with practice, students do begin both to listen to and to respond meaningfully to what their opponents have said. It helps that the opponents' contribution is sitting on the screen before them, making it harder to ignore than if it had been spoken and disappeared.

Addressing what an opponent has said can be done in quite different ways. We have identified two principal ways in which students begin to do this. The more demanding, but stronger and more effective, way to address the substance of an argument is to critique it, the argumentive goal being to weaken its force. A less effective way is to propose an alternative argument. It is a weaker argumentive strategy because it leaves the opponent's argument standing, its force unweakened. The box on the next page shows typical examples of each of these types of counterargument—the counter-critique and the counter-alternative—as we observed them in students' dialogs on the topic of capital punishment, the topic we employed in an annual assessment of how students' argumentation skills grow over time.

Argument
"I just believe that a person who has committed a serious crime/killed someone does not deserve to live because they took someone else's life."

Counter-Alternative	Counter-Critique
"There are other options for them, like a life term in jail."	"Who are we to decide who deserves what? That is God's job."

Students' dialogs during the curriculum, recall, are conducted in pairs, with a same-side pair (who hold the same position on the issue) engaging in dialog with a succession of opposing-side pairs. For assessment purposes we wanted a measure of individual students' progress. Therefore, prior to beginning the curriculum and again at the end of each year of participation, students we have worked with engage in a dialog in which they do not have a same-side partner. On their own they debate another student who holds an opposing view. Insofar as possible, these same two students discuss the capital punishment topic, a topic not included in the curriculum, at each of these points in time, so that we can examine changes in these dialogs over time.

In addition to being conducted without a same-side partner, another difference between these capital punishment (CP) dialogs and the dialogs that take place within the curriculum is that the CP dialogs are not conducted electronically. Instead, we use a method we call "Pass-the-Pad." The student holding the "Pro" CP position begins the dialog by writing his or her reason for holding this position in the top box of a pad of paper on a clipboard. The student then passes the clipboard to the opposing-position peer, who responds in writing in the box below and then returns it to the first student to respond. They are seated at a distance from one another and instructed to use the pad as their only mode of communication.

Our reason for using the handwritten Pass-the-Pad method for this assessment, instead of the electronic communication used during the curriculum itself, is that we wanted to compare students' performance to that of students who did not participate in our curriculum. Because comparison students did not have the same experience with the electronic mode of communication, we wanted to level the playing field by using the Pass-the-Pad method that neither group had experience with outside of this assessment. The method nonetheless retains one important benefit of our curriculum electronic method—enabling students to see a written running record of their dialog.

To analyze these, we examined each response a student made to the opponent, segmenting it into units if multiple ideas were expressed in a single turn. Each of these ideas was then scored based on whether it "countered" the opponent's immediately preceding statement, and, if so, in which of the two ways identified above—as a "counter-alternative" that opposes the opponent's statement by proposing an alternative argument, or as the stronger "counter-critique" that opposes the opponent's statement by critiquing it. We then calculated what proportion of a student's contributions to the dialog fell into either of these categories.

How did these proportions change during the course of students' participation in the curriculum? In Chapter 6 we summarize quantitative comparisons of the participating group's performance both over time and in relation to a comparison group who did not participate in the curriculum. In a word, the proportion of counterarguments rose among participating students but did not increase in the comparison group. Here, we illustrate this growing skill in a pair, Alicia and Roberto, who participated in the curriculum for three years and who discussed the CP topic with one another at yearly intervals.[1]

At the initial peer dialog on capital punishment (Year 0), before the curriculum began, Alicia opens with this justification for her position:

> Alicia: I am in favor of CP because if the murderer doesn't get killed they will do another crime so they should be punished.

Her more skilled opponent offers both an alternative argument and a weak critique of her position:

> Roberto: The murderer should go to jail because if he makes up for himself he can be free. Killing would just cause problems.

Alicia, ignoring both of Roberto's ideas, responds:

> Alicia: So he should be punished for what he did because you wouldn't like it if the murderer killed your parents or something. You would want him to be killed.

Alicia and Roberto's dialog on this topic at the end of Year 1 does not change greatly—the positions and justifications are similar. When the pair is assessed again at the end of year 2, Alicia makes a "pay for the crime" argument for her pro position:

> Alicia: Capital punishment should be allowed because if a person commits murder, or anything else that is very serious, then they should pay for what they did.

Now, however, we see greater dialogic skill. Alicia connects directly to Roberto's jail alternative, advancing an argument to weaken it:

> Roberto: Yes, and they should pay by serving for a long period of time in jail and not being put to death.
>
> Alicia: Why would you want to give them a second chance? They didn't give the person that they killed (murdered) a chance. They took away a life. They don't deserve a long period of time in jail.

At the final assessment at the end of year 3, Alicia remains wedded to her "pay for the crime" argument, and Roberto similarly reiterates his response to it. Alicia again directly critiques Roberto's argument. By now, however, she has strengthened her counter-critique, criticizing Roberto's alternative as both inadequate and unfair:

> Alicia: If a person commits murder, or anything else that is very serious, then they should pay for what they did.
>
> Roberto: Exactly! They should pay by spending time in prison.
>
> Alicia: What is time in prison going to do? Either way how is time in prison going to pay for what happened to the person that got murdered?

We thus see that with enough practice, even students like Alicia who begin with minimal skill gradually begin to listen to another's ideas and engage them. We see the beginnings of authentic intellectual discourse. Such evidence is important in establishing not only that the curriculum works but that it works for students who have been classified as low-ability or underachieving. Many students like Alicia who begin the program with minimal dialogic skill—they rarely acknowledge or address what their conversational partner says—gradually begin to pay attention to, to acknowledge, and finally to examine and successfully critique opposing ideas. This progress takes time, however, as we see in Alicia's case.

Keep in mind that the capital punishment topic is not part of the curriculum and Alicia and Roberto as far as we know considered it only once a year. It is not surprising, then, that on successive occasions they introduce few new ideas into their discourse, even though we can see progress in its structure. We now go on to look at how such changes transpire within the curriculum itself, as students delve deeply into the topics they talk and write about in a more concentrated fashion over many weeks.

Engaging Another's Ideas: "What Are You Saying?"

In Chapter 4, we looked at the solitary arguments students produced on the home school and juvenile justice topics. Here we observe what is very much an interactive process, with students engaging with both same-side and opposing-side peers. We look first at students' electronic dialogs with opponents and how these change over time. To facilitate comparisons with the progress in written arguments that we examined in the previous chapter, we draw illustrations from the same early and later topics sampled there, home school and juvenile justice. In each case, same-side partners work together to construct their contributions to the dialog with opposing-side pairs and must decide how to collaborate.

We begin at the very beginning, with students' initial dialog on their initial topic, home school. The following example is typical. The student pair labeled H is in favor of home school, while the pair labeled T favors the town school alternative. (Except for a few minor spelling and punctuation corrections to enhance readability, the dialogs presented here appear exactly as the pairs produced them electronically.)

H1:   hi, who is this? why are you for the town school? are you on yet?

T1:   yes im on are u on

H2:   state your case

T2:   nick should go to town school becuz he needs to learn

H3:   Even though he needs to learn he will hard time because he doesn't speak english

T3:   he can learn english over there

H4:   but his parents would still be better teachers because they know him better, by the way we're ashley and nancy

T4:   I no ur ashley and im jeffrey and eduardo if the parents are teaching him they wont get enough money to buy thier food for the family

H5:   Are you at lost for words and who is your partner the parents could work at the school or get the money from the government

T5:   No its jeffrey and eduardo what if the goverment doesnt give any money or dont give enough

H6:   is eduardo contributing?

T6:   not really this is what he wanted to say . Besides, Jeffrey is just trying to write less than usual, but the town school provides more for nick.

The dialog goes on a bit longer, but the rest is similar in form and substance. Each side offers some supporting reasons for their positions (T2, H3). More significant, they attend to one another's positions sufficiently to identify weaknesses in each of them (H3, T4). In this respect, these dialogs surpass the early capital punishment dialogs, presumably because the students are already immersed in the topic by the time they begin their dialogs. Yet note the focus is more on solving the problem—finding a way that this family could reach a solution that would work for them—than on debating the opposing alternatives.

The students' efforts, we see, occur only within a context of their preoccupation with the social dynamics of the interchange. This preoccupation with the interpersonal aspect quickly diminishes, however, as students get accustomed to the method. Here are the same two girls who argued the home school position in the dialog above now engaging in the third of their dialogs on the topic, with a third opposing pair:

T1:   he should go to town school because he will learn english and he would make friends instead of just being friends with his parents

H1:   how would he learn english if he only speaks greek

        hi sarah it's Ashley and Nancy, it would be hard for him to go to town school and do work because he doesn't speak English

T2:   By the way it is sarah and charlie and he would learn from the kids in the play ground and school from teachers

H2:   but how would he communicate at all if no one can understand him and he can't understand anyone and how would his family register for school since no one in his family speaks English

T3:   he could take a class like we take spanish and besides there are books and dvds that help you learn another language

H3:   how would he buy dvds from a store if NO ONE SPEAKS ENGLISH, also there has to be a greek teacher to translate and what if there is no greek teacher

T4:   they can hire someone to TRANSLATE!

H4:   also it's the family's choice of what to do and how will anyone translate if NO ONE KNOWS GREEK IN THE WHOLE TOWN!!!!

T5:   well, the family chose to live there
        they must know that not alot of people know greak
        and they must hire someone

H5:   his family could have chose to live there for new experences and see different parts of the world but he can still get an education at home like he did in greece.
        or they have a simple life and just homeschool him instead of going through trying to find a translator

The pairs still introduce themselves but now focus much more on the task at hand. They sustain their exchanges over a longer number of turns, and they identify weaknesses of the opposing position. But they still do not go beyond the Own-plus and Other-minus stance we identified in Chapter 4 in students' essays—here's what's right about our position and what's wrong with yours—and in this case they do so increasingly more emphatically as the dialog continues (note their use of capitalization). They identify weaknesses in the others' position (H1,2,3,4; T5) and they try to address the objections to their position that have been raised in a more sustained way than occurred in the first dialog, although still superficially (T2,3,4,5; H5) and only secondarily to advancing the merits of their own position (H4,5).

Notice, also, how the substance of this dialog reduces to the simple terms in which the H side frames it (H5): the choice is one of "finding a translator" or choosing "a simple life." As we see in the next section, one of the changes from early to later dialogs is that dilemmas cease to be seen in such simple terms. They become more than simply a problem in need of a solution. The discourse itself is also regarded differently. With time, we no longer observe dialogs conclude the way the one above did:

H9:   are you at a lost for words? do you give up?!!

[T makes no response.]

H10:   we won! Yay!

Evidence Empowers: "Supporting (and Challenging) What We Say"

We turn now to a sampling of dialogs that took place at the end of students' second year, as they addressed the juvenile justice topic. Compare these to beginning dialogs on the home school topic. A number of differences appear. Characteristics we identified in students' early dialogs have largely disappeared. Students are no longer preoccupied with the mechanics of the interchange, and their focus has shifted from solving the problem or winning the debate to engaging and addressing one another's arguments—all in all a significant shift. In addition, three further differences stand out that distinguish later dialogs from the initial ones. (A quantitative summary appears in Chapter 6.)

The most critical is the support of claims with evidence. The dialogs in the preceding section include few references to evidence. We saw in Chapters 3 and 4 that during the second year of the curriculum, students begin to recognize the key role that evidence plays in strengthening their own claims, as well as weakening those of their opponents. This increasing attention to evidence comes through clearly in students' second-year dialogs on juvenile justice. They use evidence most often to support their own claims but also to challenge those of their opponents.

Such challenges point to a second way in which these dialogs differ from students' early ones. In their electronic dialogs, students are now talking much more about the discourse, in contrast simply to engaging in it. "How do you know?" and "What is your evidence?" become frequent challenges, along with the more confrontational "You can't prove that." "That's an unwarranted assumption" also falls in this category. In the very early dialogs seen in the preceding section, we did of course observe talk about the discourse. However, it took only a surface form—identifying who the participants were and commenting on superficial aspects of their contributions. Now we observe students again talking about their discourse but in more substantive ways.

We return to this emergence of "metatalk" (talk about talk) in the next section of this chapter. We first highlight here a third characteristic that distinguishes earlier and later dialogs. In a word, we begin to see students engaging with what their opponents have to say in a deeper, more probing manner. Instead of ignoring the opponent's claim or seeking to dismiss it swiftly with a counterargument and move on, students seek to engage the opponent's position deeply, over an extended sequence rather than single exchange. This may begin with asking questions about it, probing to be sure they have understood it, yet with the ultimate goal of challenging it. The parallel challenge must also be met of dealing with the opponent's efforts to do the same with respect to one's own position.

We turn now to some examples that illustrate these changes. Typical is this question one student pair posed to their opponents, probing their argument:

> **How is that? Why would they [teen offenders] come out worse?**

Faced with probes, a common response is to make clarifications (in a way that does not damage one's own position):

> **It doesn't say if the teen is a repeat offender or not.**

Students may make the cognitive effort to engage the opponents' arguments more directly:

> **So according to your logic. . . .**

Here the intent is not simply to understand but ultimately to find a way to challenge and weaken the opposing side's position.

Despite these adversarial objectives, and ironically, perhaps the most important thing to develop from this attention to the other's arguments is that students gradually begin to see their opponents' positions in a more nuanced way, recognizing these may have some merits. We saw this in Chapter 4 in students' essays, in increasing acknowledgments of such Other-plus attributes of the opposing position. The issue comes to be seen as less black and white than it once was. This realization is a critical step in leading students to seek to connect and weigh opposing positions. We saw them do this in their increasing *However* statements in their essays. We see parallel examples of connecting opposing views in their dialogs. Here is one:

> **your saying that they will be shocked into commiting crimes again, but the evidence we provided shows that adult jail is very influential. So it is very likely that they will get rearrested.**

Deeper probing and challenging of one another's positions of course does not happen in a single exchange, and to appreciate the development that has occurred we must look at more extended excerpts from students' dialogs. Comparing these to the earlier dialogs on the home school topic, it is striking to note the overall change in tone as well as content, remembering that these are dialogs from the same group of students just 18 months later.

Here now is a dialog that reflects all the developments we have noted. The student pair labeled A is in favor of teens being served in the adult system, while the pair labeled J favors a juvenile justice system. Statements citing evidence appear in italics. Metalevel statements about evidence or arguments appear in bold. Again, except for a few spelling and punctuation corrections to enhance readability, the dialogs appear exactly as the pairs conveyed them electronically to the opposing pair.

> **A1:** juveniles should be trialed as adults that commit serious crimes. adult prisons can help juveniles from continuing to commit crimes. *there is a 30% that people who get out of jail do not commit crimes again*
>
> **J1:** Yes, but a juvinile's mind is more permeable. They may get influenced by bad adults in jail. Furthurmore, they will not get educated as well in ADULT jail because there are no teachers for children there. Even if they do get educated there, it will not be as good as the education that Juvi has to offer.
>
> **A2:** well, juvenile centers do offer better aspects like education and rehabilitation. However, adult prisons offer rehabilitation and job training programs. any way both places have negative influences. they both have violence.

J2:   Maybe, but the children abuse other children, which gives them a chance to fight back. Also, studies show that *70% of people who come out of adult jail are rearrested*. This shows that Adult jail is worse as an influence for juvis.

A3:   **you can't prove that.** Juvi records are not available. records are sealed after teens reach 18. so you can't compare them.

J3:   **we have evidence**

A4:   **where is it? Tell us then**

Notable in this dialog is the continuity from beginning to end that was largely missing in students' early dialogs. Each contribution connects to the preceding one. Though J does not start off strongly, ducking A's opening argument that the adult system can reduce recidivism, J later makes two arguments against it (bad influence, no teachers). Also, importantly, A raises a potential strength of J's position (juveniles need education) and goes on to connect the two positions in this regard in a comparative statement. In A2, A maintains this comparative stance as well as that of recognizing both positive and negative aspects of a position, more explicitly and exhaustively than did J, in fact identifying both pros and cons of both positions. In J2, J then reverts to an oppositional stance, introducing a new Own-plus argument, but J maintains the comparative stance and draws on evidence. Notice, interestingly, that J in fact draws on the same evidence that A opened with, but reframes it (70 percent rearrested, versus A's statement that 30 percent are not rearrested) to different ends. In A3, A then engages J's argument directly, challenging it on lack-of-evidence grounds, and the remainder of the dialog is focused on this metalevel exchange about evidence.

In the following dialog between two other pairs discussing the same topic, the pair favoring the adult court position (again identified as A) starts strongly, explaining its position's potential implications and including relevant evidence. The opposing side J provides a clarification that affects A's argument, as well as providing own-side evidence for the J position and taking a comparative perspective. In A2, A acknowledges and interprets the opponents' evidence and evaluates its implications for the opposing argument it supports. In this dialog as in the preceding one, we thus see the participants staying very much "on task" in their discourse, their argumentive task being to address one another's claims. They recognize the need to support their claims with evidence. Their dialog is well sustained. It almost entirely remains connected, rarely letting the opponent's statements go unaddressed. Again, evidence appears in italics and metalevel statements in bold.

A1:   Juveniles should be tried in adult court if they're repeat offenders. Being a repeat offender shows that the delinquent has not learned their lesson and that they have a potential to become felons in the near future. Therefore, they deserve a harsher punishment, and *studies have shown that adult prison is stricter than juvenile prison* (a.k.a. Juvie). Not only that, but teenagers should be old enough to comprehend the consequences of their actions.

J1:   However, **it does not specify if the teen is a repeat offender or not.** It only asks if they should be tried in a separate system. Adult prison is much harsher than juvenile prison and juvie might be like a warning for them which can possibly keep them from becoming repeat offenders and help better their lives. Also, *the prefrontal cortex is not fully developed until the age of 25* so teens still have time.

A2 :   Even if teens still have time as you say, that does not indicate that teens have the comprehension of a 1-year-old. Even my 3-year-old niece knows that if someone dies, they are gone forever. Basically everyone over the age of 2 knows that killing and taking others' possessions is wrong. Some teens may be mature but act innocent so a judge/jury won't give them a corresponding sentence.

J2:   **There is no proven evidence for your statement and you are using examples from your personal life that might not apply to everyone. Also, teens shouldn't be held completely responsible for their punishments. Sometimes teens have trouble at home and reflect their parents and to bring up the point again** *teens minds are not fully developed*, **unlike adults who know much better. How do they know if they are acting innocent or not?**

A3:   **I said "may", which indicates that I do not know if they are acting innocent or not.** Even if they are not acting innocent as I suggested, they might get out through bail without truly learning their lesson. Some teenagers may have that problem but not all teens may have that problem.

Perhaps of greatest interest in this dialog is what the participants increasingly focus on as the dialog continues—"metatalk" about discourse, to which we now turn.

Discourse about Discourse

In the preceding dialog, we see the talk turn to "what counts" as evidence and what kinds of claims different kinds of evidence can support. More fundamentally, how does anyone know something for sure? What status do opinions have, and are some better than others? This "metatalk" is very revealing of what students come to understand as the rules of intellectual discourse. The remarkable achievement reflected in such talk is not just students' recognition that these are important matters, but their awareness that they are matters that need to be addressed and negotiated with one another, with agreement reached regarding shared norms that will govern their interaction.

These were not isolated achievements we saw. Recognition of the critical role of evidence and the demand for it were most common, reflected in these typical discourse moves against the opponent:

You need evidence to support your argument.

And more strongly:

Your argument is faulty. There is no evidence.

Another student pair, however, criticized their opponents on different grounds:

You are only looking at one perspective, which is the negative side of adult systems. You aren't looking at it both ways. Therefore, you never know the positive effect of adult prison. The positive effects of adult prison is that they are more strict, therefore they learn there lesson better.

Later they go on to put it more sweepingly:

I know what side you're on, but what I'm saying is that you aren't seeing both sides of the argument.

Clearly these students are learning valuable things from their engagement with one another, in many ways but specifically and explicitly in this case regarding the norms of discourse. How have they come to believe, as these students tell their peers, that it is important to "look at it both ways?" In the final chapter we reflect on this influence students have on one another as they participate as members of a peer group that develops shared norms of discourse. First, it remains to note that this influence is not limited in our curriculum to the electronic dialogs students conduct. In addition, they communicate with one another in the small-group work before and after the dialogs, but also during the dialogs themselves, as same-side partners collaborate in conducting the dialogs. Pairs had plenty to say to one another as they planned what to say, waited for responses from their opponents, and then reflected on the responses they received. We were able to unobtrusively audiorecord some of their collaboration. It is impossible to briefly summarize the wide range of ways in which we observed partners supporting one another, but in the box below we provide a sampling.

How Do Partners Support Each Other? Questioning, Planning, Evaluating

What should we start out with?

I'm just thinking of the other side, of what they're gonna say.

Can you read me that again, their counter?

What does that mean?

That's not making any sense.

We don't know.

Is there any evidence for this?

But we need to use evidence.

Why should we use that evidence?

Did they use any evidence for that?

How's that helping them?

What do you think?

So what can we write?

But it doesn't connect to what they said.

We should have written something else.

You just improved that argument.

What is clear is that the within-pair discourse in our curriculum is as much a source of students' gains as is the opposing-pair discourse. Indeed, in one comparison we did in which students conducted their electronic dialogs without a same-side partner, the decline in students' engagement and performance was so great that we quickly ended it after one topic. Clearly, then, both collaborative (same-side) and adversarial (opposing-side) discourse have roles to play. In the next chapter we summarize evidence documenting their effects on individual performance.

Notes

1. Adapted from material presented by A. Crowell & D. Kuhn (2014), in the article "Developing dialogic argumentation skills: A three-year intervention study," *Journal of Cognition and Development.*

Chapter 6

■ ■ ■

Assessing Curriculum Outcomes

HOW CAN WE BE SURE WHAT STUDENTS GAIN FROM THE CURRICULUM WE HAVE DESCRIBED? Are the benefits great enough to justify the time invested? In this chapter, we report quantitatively on intellectual outcomes among groups of middle-schoolers we followed as they participated in the curriculum. The chapter serves two potential purposes. One is to provide answers to the above questions for readers who would like to have them. The other is to describe the assessment tools we used to measure these gains. These tools may be useful for teachers who wish to assess gains in their own students.

Participant and Comparison Groups

The students whose progress we have studied come from three schools in New York City in the neighborhood surrounding Columbia University, where residents range from middle to lower class. Two of the three groups attend public schools and one private. The private school is a K–8 school, and one of the public schools, Columbia Secondary School, is a grade 6–12 school, both affiliated with Columbia University. The other public middle school is nearby. The private school is well equipped with resources, while the two public schools struggle with a scarcity of funds. Demographically each of the three schools serves diverse populations, with a significant proportion of African-American and Hispanic students and students from low-income families. The proportion of low-income students is higher in the two public schools, with 60 percent or more qualifying for free or reduced-price lunch.

In total, 14 classes of 30-plus students each participated in the curriculum and in the associated assessments we report on here. Most of the classes participated for two years, five for only one year, and one for three years (allowing us to assess the "value added" of an additional year of participation). Twelve of the 14 classes came from the five successive entering classes of Columbia Secondary School between 2007 and 2011. These are the classes that provide the data we report on here. Publications reporting on other schools are listed at the end of the chapter.[1] Also included is the source for a report on implementation of a version of the curriculum with a more specialized population, residents of a juvenile detention center.[2] The articles listed at the end of the chapter contain full statistical and other technical details.

The Columbia Secondary classes provided an extraordinarily valuable sample for evaluating the effects of the curriculum during the five-year period our reporting covers. Each entering 6th-grade cohort at the school comprises roughly 96 students divided into three sections equivalent with respect to demographic characteristics and academic standing. Our argumentation curriculum was situated in a twice-weekly free-standing class (rather than included within the curriculum of a customary school subject) that all students enrolled in each year. It was identified as a course in philosophy. Among each cohort, only two of the three sections (and in two of the five years only one of the three) participated in our curriculum.

The remaining class sections enrolled in a parallel class taught by regular school faculty, also identified as a class in philosophy. It followed a more traditional whole-class discussion format, with required writing assignments and some role-playing activities. These classes were loosely based on a Philosophy for Children[3] model, and students discussed many of the same topics as students in our curriculum, although without the focused pair dialogs, electronic discourse, or structured debates that our curriculum features. Instead, they focused on whole-class discussion and frequent essay writing (more than students participating in our curriculum). We conducted initial and final assessments with these classes as well, thus allowing for a close comparison of cognitive outcomes for the two groups.

The comparison is ideal because the students who participated in our curriculum and those in the comparison classes came from the same overall school environment. All of their other classes were identical, and the required philosophy course was equivalent in time and work investment. This structure is very different from the more typical "business as usual" experimental/control comparison, in which control students get no special experience while the experimental students do something new and different. We were thus able to closely compare the gains observed among our students relative to gains among the comparison students. This enabled us to conclude with considerable confidence that the differences observed could be attributed to experiences specific to our curriculum. Other explanations could be eliminated, such as extra attention paid to the experimental group (since the classes in philosophy were characterized as new and innovative to parents and students from all classes) or to preexisting differences between the two groups (since assignment to classes had been done randomly).

For the first four years, our dialogic curriculum was delivered entirely by our research staff, with much of this work supported by funding from the U.S. Institute of Education Sciences, while the control curriculum was delivered by school faculty. During the fifth year, three of the first-year sections of our curriculum were taught by a member of the school faculty who volunteered for the assignment, with support and consultation by our team. We saw this as a next and critical step in establishing that our curriculum is deliverable by regular teachers.

We turn now to the outcomes we assessed. They fall into two broad categories, reflecting the distinction we introduced in Chapter 1 between dialogic argumentation and individual argumentive productions (whether written or oral). We begin with assessments of dialogic argumentation, even though teachers reading this book are likely to be most interested in the effects of the curriculum on students' argumentive writing. Students write argumentive essays as part of the curriculum, but the predominant activity is dialogic. Students' performance on assessments of dialogic skill can therefore be thought of as primary outcomes, while their performance on individual argumentive essays is a measure of transfer or generalization of the primary outcomes to other related skills.

Our report focuses on assessments conducted just before the curriculum began and annually thereafter. In all cases, assessment of students in the comparison group was conducted at the same times. Because progress is typically very gradual, we concentrate on final outcome assessments.

Dialogic Argumentation

Our foremost goal for participating students, and the initial objective of the curriculum, was to get them first to listen and second to respond to one another. As we have noted throughout, this does not come naturally. In a dialogic context, young people (and even many older ones) are most focused on saying what they themselves have to say.

We therefore focused on how students responded to an opponent's statement. Did they ignore it, continuing with what they had been saying, or did they turn the conversation in a new direction? Or did they acknowledge what the opponent said, by addressing it in some manner?

In Chapter 5, we identified two principal ways in which this could be accomplished. The stronger, more effective of the two—which we called a counter-critique—is to critique what the opponent has said, the argumentive goal being to weaken its force.

The less effective strategy, called a counter-alternative, is to oppose the statement but to do so by proposing an alternative argument. This is a weaker argumentive strategy because it leaves the opponent's argument standing, its force unweakened. In Chapter 5 we included examples of each of these and an illustration of change over time for one pair of students. We noted how these responses to the opponent changed in form as this pair discussed the same topic (capital punishment) at annual assessments.

We conducted this same analysis for a group of 56 students who participated in the curriculum over multiple years and compared their progress to a group of 23 students who participated in the alternative philosophy curriculum.[4] For assessment purposes we wanted a measure of individual students' progress. Therefore, at the outset and annually thereafter, we assessed pairs of students in both groups as they debated the capital punishment topic, a topic not included in the curriculum. (The pair held opposing views on the topic and insofar as possible they remained a pair throughout.) The pair conducted the dialog in writing, using the "Pass-the-Pad" method described in Chapter 5. This written document was their only mode of communication.

We examined each response a student made to the opponent in the Pass-the-Pad document, segmenting it into units if multiple ideas were expressed in a single turn. Each of these ideas was scored according to whether it "countered" the opponent's immediately preceding statement in either of the two ways identified earlier—as a counter-alternative that opposes the opponent's statement by proposing an alternative argument or as the stronger counter-critique that opposes the opponent's statement and directly critiques it. We then calculated what proportion of a student's statements fell into either of these categories at each assessment.

These proportions rose with each yearly assessment among the participating group but not among the comparison group. Figure 6-1 shows proportions for total counterarguments (of either the counter-alternative or counter-critique type), while Figure 6-2 shows these proportions for the stronger counter-critiques. As comparison of the two figures shows, it is mainly the simpler counter-alternative arguments that become more prevalent during the first year, while counter-critiques do not rise until the second year and least overall gain appears during the third year. When these gains are broken down by initial skill level, however, the third of the dialogic group that showed least skill at the initial assessment continue to improve during the third year, indicating that the program continued to be of benefit to them. Indeed, even this least able group, after sustained engagement in argumentation with peers, were able to reach a proportion of direct counterargument of almost 50 percent, almost equivalent to that of their peers who began their participation with more initial skill.

These findings are important in establishing not only that the curriculum works but that it works for low-ability students. Many students, like Alicia, whose capital punishment dialogs are illustrated in Chapter 5, begin the program with no dialogic skill—never acknowledging or addressing what their conversational partner has to say. Yet in significant numbers these students gradually begin to pay attention to, acknowledge, and finally examine and successfully critique opposing ideas. We are confident in our claim that they have become capable of partaking in authentic intellectual discourse.

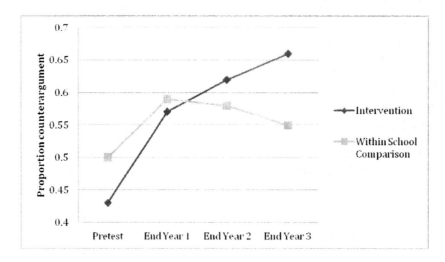

Figure 6-1. Average Proportion Total Counterargument Use

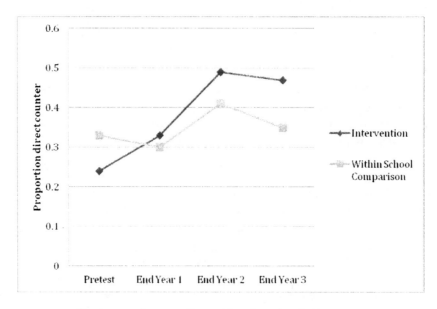

Figure 6-2. Average Proportion Counter-Critique Use

Evaluating Argumentation

In Chapter 1 we made the case that evaluating arguments is more cognitively demanding than producing them. We therefore wanted to ask whether students' progress in producing authentic dialogic argumentation would extend to skill in evaluating such argumentation. In contrast to the dialogic production task just described, we did not present this task until students had completed the curriculum, as we anticipated that the skills entailed would take some time to develop. In an individual paper-and-pencil task, we presented 61 eighth-grade students who had completed two or three years in our curriculum and 21 eighth-graders who had spent the same amount of time in the comparison philosophy curriculum with a written copy of the following dialog:

Pat: Schools should do away with uniforms. They are a bad idea.

Lee: I think students should have to wear uniforms because then they all look neat and orderly and it's better for learning.

Pat: Students get tired of wearing the same thing every day. They like to express themselves by looking different from one another. It shows their personality.

Lee: They have other ways to make themselves look different besides clothing.

Pat: Some families don't have the money to buy uniforms.

Lee: Schools usually have a fund for families who need help with school expenses.

The student's task was to evaluate each contribution to the dialog, beginning with Lee's first statement, as either a Good, Weak, or Poor response, and then explain their judgment. This is a demanding metalevel task in that the respondent must inhibit the inclination to simply evaluate the content of the statement but instead focus on the statement as a discourse move, considering the relation of the statement to the opponent's preceding statement. Thus, the task is one of evaluating argumentation, not the more common task of evaluating an individual argument.

Students found the task difficult and a number succumbed to evaluating the argument itself (e.g., Lee's argument is good because that's a good reason). However, the group participating in the curriculum was overall significantly more capable in performing this task than was the comparison group.[5] Among the participating group, significantly more students (33 percent) were successful in evaluating Lee's opening statement in relation to Pat's preceding one (e.g., It challenges Pat's statement), than the 10 percent among the comparison group. Pat's next contribution similarly was successfully evaluated as good (in countering Lee's preceding statement) by 38 percent of the participating group but none of the comparison group.

The fourth and sixth contributions (both by Lee) elicited similar differences between the groups, with significantly more students in the participating group noting the successful countering function of the statement. The fifth contribution to the dialog (Pat's final one) is the most challenging of all to evaluate as it requires noting a failure, or missed opportunity, to make a counterargument against the preceding contribution. Here, 42 percent of the participating group correctly pointed this out and rated the contribution as poor, compared to 20 percent of the comparison group.

The participating group's performance is far from perfect. Only 9.8 percent of this group made appropriate judgments for all of the five they were asked to judge. For four of the five, 41.0 percent did so; for three of the five, 67.2 percent did so; and for two of the five, 86.9 percent did so. In the comparison group, no students showed more than two successful responses, with 54.6 percent showing none. The comparison makes it clear that the group who participated in the dialogic curriculum has made significant progress in understanding the requirements of argumentive discourse and judging it appropriately.

Constructing Argumentation

An even more challenging task we asked eighth graders to perform was to construct their own excerpt of argumentive discourse between two opponents (see box on page 75). In other words, the student had to invent both persons' contributions. Responses of 45 participant-group students and 25 comparison-group students who had completed either two or three years in either our curriculum or the comparison curriculum were examined.

We deliberately kept the content lean and in a knowledge realm that respondents could deal with comfortably based on their knowledge of urban life. To be assessed favorably, the contributions to the dialog that the student constructed needed to be comparative, with Diaz's qualifications evaluated in relation to Cruz's and vice versa. An absolute judgment about the merit of one candidate would be less informative. We therefore looked for indications of these comparative claims in students' constructed dialogs. Furthermore, merit needed to be defined in relation to criteria, presented as the needs or demands the candidate should be able to address (the city's problems). The constructor of a strong argument in support of one candidate over the other had to recognize that the candidates' stated plans were the only available evidence provided and appreciate the need to draw on them to support (or weaken) argumentive claims regarding each candidate's comparative strength. We therefore examined the extent to which the student drew on these candidate statements of intention as evidence to support the arguer's claim and also the extent to which they did so comparatively, addressing not only the strengths of one arguer's preferred candidate but also the relative weaknesses of the opponent's preferred candidate. In addition, we examined whether the constructor drew on this available evidence in a comprehensive or integrated manner, rather than a piecemeal one, recognizing that a decisive argument supporting one candidate over the other could be made only if the evidence were employed comprehensively. (The evidence was constructed such that some of the identified issues were addressed by both candidates, whereas others were addressed by only one; some of the candidates' proposed actions were not linked to an identified need.)

We first coded each of the statements in a student's constructed dialog using largely the same coding scheme we had used in coding students' own discourse.[5] "Unconnected" was the most frequent category among the comparison group (average of 40 percent of statements), while "counter-critique" was the most frequent among the participating group (57 percent).

The purpose of applying a second coding scheme to constructed dialogs was to portray how evidence is used as a resource for argumentation in these dialogs. In other words, what do the constructed dialogs reflect regarding students' understanding of the role of evidence in argument? Would students recognize the need to include evidence as a basis for supporting the claims made by each contributor? All students sometimes incorporated evidence in their constructed dialogs, although students in the participating group did so more frequently. An average of 86 percent of a student's constructed dialog units among the participating group and 68 percent of a student's constructed dialog units among the comparison group included a reference to evidence (i.e., to a candidate's claim).

What use was made of this evidence in the constructed dialogs? Both groups commonly mentioned a single piece of positive evidence as support for a claim. However, the participating group were more likely to make use of evidence in other ways as well. First, they more often included statements that used evidence to support a claim against one of the candidates, with averages of 21 percent among the participating group versus 11 percent among the comparison group. This use of evidence predominantly to support rather than argue against a claim is consistent with what we observed in middle school students' own discourse, as we note shortly.

Secondly, the participating group's dialog units were more likely to use evidence in an integrative way (i.e., to draw on multiple pieces of evidence to support a claim either for or against one candidate), with an average of 32 percent of total units among the participating group versus 17 percent among the comparison group. Finally, constructed dialogs that contained only single, isolated pieces of supportive evidence were more common in the comparison group (59 percent) than in the participating group (39 percent). The constructed dialogs in the box on page 76 illustrate the contrast between a dialog that does not show mastery in these respects and one that does.[5]

Discourse Construction Assessment

Ana Cruz and Maria Diaz are running for mayor of their troubled large city. Among the city's problems are high housing costs, teen crime, traffic, school dropout, and unemployment. Chuck and Doug are TV commentators arguing about who is the better candidate. Write a script of what they might say. Both of them are experts on the city, and they are both expert arguers and evenly matched. So your script should present the most well-argued debate you can construct.

Begin your script like this:

> **CHUCK: Cruz should be elected mayor because she'll do better than Diaz.**
>
> **DOUG: I disagree, because xxxxxx**

Then continue their argument, filling in what each one might say:

> **CHUCK: xxxxxx**
>
> **DOUG: xxxxxxx**
>
> **CHUCK: xxxxxx etc.**

Here is some information about Cruz' positions. She promises to:

- create job training programs
- expand city parks
- raise teachers' pay
- open walk-in health clinics
- reduce rents
- impose a teen curfew
- employ senior citizens in city schools

Here is some information about Diaz' positions. She promises to:

- improve public transportation
- open more centers for senior citizens
- revise the high school curriculum
- build a new athletic stadium
- improve health care
- build more housing

(You are not required to include all these topics in your script.)

Illustrations of Low-End and High-End Constructed Dialogs

Low-End Dialog

Chuck: Cruz will create job training programs.

Doug: Well Cruz also wants to have teen curfew, take me back to World War II Germany. However Diaz will help teens by improving the high school system.

Chuck: Cruz will reduce rent.

Doug: Diaz will open centers for senior citizens.

Chuck: Cruz will raise teachers' pay.

Doug: Diaz will build a new athletic stadium.

Chuck: Cruz will create open, walk-in clinics.

Doug: Well I now agree that Diaz is better for mayor.

High-End Dialog

Doug: Cruz's ideas are more social and domestic. Diaz's ideas are more realistic and will help more people in the community.

Chuck: Even though Diaz's plan will further help the community, Cruz's plan will allow for the government to have more control over what happens.

Doug: The government may have more control, but Cruz has no control over what she is trying to accomplish, like imposing curfew. That is not up to her, it is up to the parents to decide.

Chuck: She can try to convince parents to impose curfew. Making kids have curfew may lower crime rates and dropout rates.

Doug: How sure are you that this will actually help. I don't quite understand why Cruz's ideas will help the community as a whole and promote its growth and well-being.

Chuck: She does have good ideas, like expanding city parks and creating job training programs.

Doug: She may have those, but what exactly is the point of raising teacher's pay or employing senior citizens in schools? While Diaz's promises improve many public facilities–transportation and health care.

Chuck: What else does she "promise" to do, because from what I know she is only trying to improve things, and not for growth.

Doug: Do you really think that it's easy for the governor to do so many things at once? Cruz has lots of ideas she wants to make a reality, but if you think about it, they don't help as much as you think it will. They won't even help those who need it. Diaz hopes to open more senior citizen centers, revise h.s. curriculum, build new athletic stadium, build more housing and many more. Each of these is also associated with each one of our problems that we are currently facing. These solutions may be harder to obtain, but they are better because they help the larger community.

In sum, performance on both the argumentation evaluation and constructed argumentation tasks indicates that the participating group, relative to the comparison group, had achieved deeper understanding of the discourse norm that interlocutors should address each other's points and evaluate them critically. The same can be said for norms regarding the need to draw on evidence and to do so in a comprehensive rather than fragmentary or unilateral manner. We thus regard these two post-intervention assessments as further supporting the claim that students participating in our curriculum not only made gains in strategic skill as a result of argument practice but also made gains on a meta-strategic level. Participating students called on and applied their new knowledge about argumentation in more challenging tasks beyond those presented within the intervention.

Argumentive Writing

We thus see the beginnings of authentic intellectual discourse in multiple forms—production, evaluation, and construction. The question educators are most likely to want an answer to at this point, however, is this: Do these gains transfer to the more familiar—and critical—one in educational settings, one in which students must express their own views in individual expository writing?

We have already explored the question in Chapter 4, following students in the progress they made in their individual writing assignments within the curriculum. In completing these assignments, students had the benefit of having just completed an intensive engagement with the topic, including the culminating activities of the highly motivating Showdown and the debrief analysis of it. We thus wanted to know whether any gains they showed in their written work would be confined to writing on these well-studied topics.

We therefore administered at each assessment point an additional writing assignment on a topic that was not part of the curriculum. For purposes of close comparison, we kept the topic of this essay assessment the same over time, to be able to more precisely gauge students' gains. These essays were written in class under controlled conditions, at about the same time as the capital punishment dialogic assessment—once at the outset of the curriculum and again at the end of each year of participation thereafter. Like the dialogic assessments, this essay assessment was also administered to the comparison classes not participating in the curriculum, allowing a close comparison of skill. The students we report on here are from the same group whose progress in dialogic argumentation we reported on earlier in this chapter.

The annual essay assessment is perhaps the most challenging test of student gains in argumentive writing since the topic was not one with which they had been deeply engaged. Would they show superior argumentive writing relative to a comparison group who had more writing practice but who, like the participating group, had no particular background with respect to the topic?

The topic we chose for students to write about proved to be a very rich one. Here it is:

> **The new Columbia Town School has to decide how to pay its teachers. Some think every teacher should get the same pay. Others think that teachers should be paid according to how much experience they have, with teachers getting more pay for each year of teaching experience they have. Which do you think is the better plan and why?**

This essay prompt elicits a wide range of arguments on both sides. It is one that has a connection to students' experience, but it poses a question students are unlikely to have been asked before. Nor are they likely to address it in or out of school during the intervals between our assessments, an important consideration given that we wished to assess changes in students' responses in repeated assessments over a three-year period. Excerpts from these essays appear in Table 6-1.

Results of our analysis of these essays are summarized in Table 6-2. Although a few students simply repeated their position as a reason (first row in Table 6-1), almost all offered at least one reason in support of their position (second row in Table 6-1). Our interest is in whether they do any more than this. Figure 6-3 shows the average number of what we called dual-perspective arguments made at each time point, while Table 6-2 shows the proportion of students making any arguments of this type.[6]

A dual-perspective argument is so called because it adds to the writer's own-side supporting argument an argument that addresses the opposing position. As illustrated in Table 6-1, this is almost always an argument that critiques the opposing position, characterizing a weakness or drawback it possesses (what we labeled O– in the topic essays described in Chapter 4). An essay composed entirely of own-side supporting arguments and opposing-side critiquing arguments can thus be advanced as a unified whole, with no conflict or need for reconciliation of opposing views: My position is better, the other position is worse; my position should prevail, and that ends the matter. There are, however, other potential arguments that can be made—namely those that identify weaknesses or drawbacks of my position and/or virtues or advantages of the opposing position (labeled M– and O+ in Chapter 4). In this case, arguments weigh in opposing directions and an effort at reconciliation, or at least relative weighing of the two sides, is warranted. An essay meeting these criteria falls in the integrative category.

Table 6-1. Excerpts from Teacher Pay Essays[6]

Argument Type	Examples	
	Equal Pay is Preferred Option	**Experience-Based Pay is Preferred Option**
No argument	All the teachers should get the same pay because it shouldn't depend on how experienced you are as a teacher that determines how much you get paid.	More experienced teachers should get paid more because if a new teacher just came into the school and another teacher has been working there for years the more experienced teacher should get more money.
Own-side only (includes only positives of preferred option)	Teachers should get paid the same amount because they are all going to teach a subject that is going to help the children's education in some way.	Teachers with more experience should get paid more because they are the ones that worked hard to get in the position they're in.
	I think all teachers should get the same pay because think how hard ALL teachers work.	Experienced teachers should get more pay because of the skills they have, because they have more to offer the students.
Dual perspective (includes negatives of other option)	If teachers were paid according to experience, this would create conflict for the teachers because there would be a very large disagreement on how much each teacher is getting paid.	If new teachers got the same pay, experienced teachers would get fed up and quit.
	Unequal pay wouldn't be good because experienced teachers have already been paid for their previous years of teaching; it would be like paying them twice.	If experienced teachers got the same pay as new teachers, they would feel like it was unfair and not want to help out the new teachers.
	The new teachers might not even want to teach at a school that gives them so little pay; then how will you get new teachers?	
Integrative perspective (includes negatives of preferred option or positives of other option)	Experienced-based pay may seem fair to those who have taught for a long time [positive other]. But not for the new teachers who do just as much as everyone else [negative other].	Although it does seem unfair the school is basing your salary on age [negative own], it's a clever way to keep good teachers for a longer time [positive own].

**Table 6-2. Percentages of Students Making Dual-Perspective and
Integrative Arguments on Teacher Pay Essay[6]**

	Initial		Year 1		Year 2		Year 3	
	E	C	E	C	E	C	E	C
Percentage of participants making any dual-perspective arguments	35	35	67	38	79	19	79	29
Percentage of participants making any integrative arguments	00	00	00	00	00	00	30	00

Note. E=Experimental; C=Comparison.

As Figure 6-3 and Table 6-2 show, the majority of students participating in the curriculum begin to make dual-perspective arguments by the end of year 1. They do not begin to make integrative arguments, however, until year 3. Comparison-group students, in contrast, show no evidence of gains in either respect. Thus, progress in argumentive essays is evident, even though it is far from complete. Nor does it proceed as rapidly as we observed in Chapter 4 in the case of the topic essays, where students had sustained experience with and deep investment in the topic.

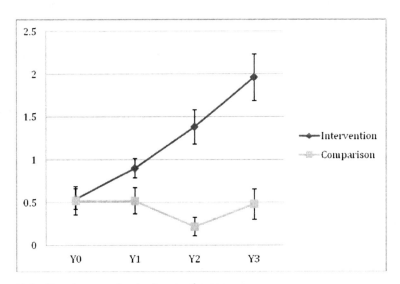

Note. Error bars = standard error of mean.

Figure 6-3. Mean Number of Dual-Perspective Arguments on Teacher Pay Essay[6]

A further key aspect of students' argumentive essays that we addressed in Chapter 4 is their use of evidence to support claims. In this regard we report here on a different group (of classes from two later cohorts at Columbia Secondary School) and a different essay topic, to separate this analysis from an analysis of progress on the annual teacher pay essays. For this topic, whether cigarette sales should be banned, we provided the list shown in Chapter 4 of information that might be of help to them in writing their essays. We did not expect use of evidence to improve measurably until the second year, when it begins to be emphasized in the curriculum, and this prediction was confirmed. Students who had thus far completed only the first year of the curriculum showed no greater use of evidence in their essays (or in their dialogs within the curriculum) than did a comparison group who had not participated in the curriculum.[7] After two years in the curriculum, however, the use of evidence surpassed that of students who had completed one or no years. Two-year participants supported an average of 79.4% of claims with evidence in their essays, compared to 56.5% in the one-year and no-year groups combined. Similarly in dialogs, corresponding percentages, although lower, were significantly different for the two groups, 42.3% vs. 30.7%. Moreover, in another comparison, another group (see Chapter 4) were not asked to write the smoking essay until one year after the curriculum concluded, and their use of evidence in their essays continued to significantly exceed that of the comparison group.

Conclusions

Despite their progress in using evidence, it is worth noting that when students (regardless of group) used evidence in their essays, they were much more likely to use it to support claims favorable to their own positions than to use it to weaken claims favorable to the opposing position. Progress over time in this respect did not appear, although we have found that a prompt before writing, asking the student to try to weaken the opponent's position, does increase the use of evidence for this purpose. Hence, it appears to be not the competence that students lack, but rather the awareness of this argumentive strategy as a potentially effective one.

A broader conclusion to be drawn is that the evidence of progress presented in this chapter is far from evidence that students have attained a high level of competence with little room for further progress. To the contrary, what we have portrayed here are solid signs of a foundation for the argumentive skills that it will benefit students to master. Without them, their futures are constrained in numerous respects. We return to this claim in the final chapter.

In conclusion, summarized in this chapter is the evidence to support our most central claim. Closely matched comparison groups of middle-school students participated in a curriculum whose duration and involvement was equivalent to that of our dialogic curriculum. The major difference was its lack of focus on peer-to-peer dialog, whereas our curriculum is centered around such dialog. Hence, it is in large part this dialogic aspect of the curriculum that we can take to be responsible for the greater skill development shown by students participating in the dialogic curriculum. We turn finally in the next chapter to broader implications.

Notes

1. Kuhn, D., Goh, W., Iordanou, K., & Shaenfield, D. (2008). Arguing on the computer: A microgenetic study of developing argument skills in a computer-supported environment. *Child Development, 79*, 1311–1329.

2. DeFuccio, M., Kuhn, D., Udell, W., & Callender, K. (2009). Developing argument skills in severely disadvantaged adolescent males in a residential setting. *Applied Developmental Science, 13*, 30–41.

3. Lipman, M. (1980). *Philosophy in the classroom*. Philadelphia: Temple University Press.

4. Crowell, A., & Kuhn, D. (2014). Developing dialogic argumentation skills: A three-year intervention study. *Journal of Cognition and Development.*

5. Kuhn, D., Zillmer, N., Crowell, A., & Zavala, J. (2013). Developing norms of argumentation: Metacognitive, epistemological, and social dimensions of developing argumentive competence. *Cognition & Instruction, 31 (4)*, 456–496.

6. Kuhn, D., & Crowell, A. (2011). Dialogic argumentation as a vehicle for developing young adolescents' thinking. *Psychological Science, 22*, 545—552.

7. Moore, W. (2012). The role of evidence in argumentation. Unpublished doctoral dissertation. Teachers College, Columbia University.

Chapter 7

■ ■ ■

Argument in the Precollege Curriculum

IN THE PRECEDING CHAPTERS we have described a dialog-centered argument curriculum, along with guidelines for implementing it in forms that can range from a multiyear fixture of the curriculum to a single unit inserted into a middle-school or high-school social studies, ELA, or science curriculum. One thing we have not done is addressed how a teacher might find the time to do any of these. The demands on teachers, and on students, are intense these days. Whether a school is an academically high-functioning or a struggling one, there are rarely any open spots in the curriculum to fit in anything new, and teachers and principals become uneasy about what it would have to replace.

If they are to find the time, teachers and administrators will need to be able to justify to themselves and to others that the activity we have described warrants the time invested. Do students have as much to gain from this investment as from the many alternatives competing for classroom time?

In this chapter we summarize the reasons for an affirmative answer to this question. Three reasons immediately present themselves: First, the approach is educationally sound. Second, it has been shown to produce desired outcomes. Third, its objectives are prominent in the new Common Core and Next Generation Science Standards.

Both qualitative and quantitative evidence that the approach works, and the kinds and patterns of change it produces, have been portrayed in the preceding chapters. Students' argumentative discourse with peers gradually becomes stronger with the sustained practice the curriculum provides, and this enhanced skill transfers to the crucial academic context of individual expository writing. The forms that this evolving competence takes are portrayed in Chapters 4 and 5 and summarized quantitatively in Chapter 6.

The fact that the approach is successful in achieving its goals when it is implemented falls short of telling us whether it is worth implementing. Why should we think that it is? Here, perhaps, we need only turn to the Common Core Standards. These tell us clearly and consistently that students must be able to construct and comprehend arguments in increasingly complex forms as they progress through the grades. For educators on the front lines charged with achieving these standards, this may be reason enough to adopt a method shown to do this. However, many educators—and we are among them—wish to look beyond the standards for reasons. We do just that in this chapter, asking how an argumentation curriculum like this one stands to benefit students broadly.

Given that this is a book about argumentation, we would be remiss if we did not consider arguments against this approach. We do that in this chapter as well.

Why Not?

We in fact turn to arguments against the approach first, because one of them takes precedence over any other consideration. It is the possibility that some teachers will not feel at ease with the approach and will find it too challenging to implement. To the extent this is the case, this weakness is a fatal one, for teachers will not choose to adopt a curriculum they do not feel comfortable using and will look for other ways to achieve the same goals.

What is it about the curriculum that might make it challenging to implement? One reason is that it asks teachers to play a role many will have little experience with—the role of coach, standing back and letting students do the work, offering support on an as-needed basis. Students participating in our curriculum do not look to the teacher as the sole source of knowledge. A consequence is that they take much greater responsibility for their own activities and progress, figuring out what their objectives are and how they are going to meet them.

Shifting one's role from being at the center of what goes on in the classroom may at first lessen teachers' confidence that they are doing their job. To assume the coach role, teachers will need to relinquish some control over what is happening in their classroom. While monitoring and facilitating multiple exchanges, they cannot expect to hear every exchange that takes place among their students, nor should they try.

A teacher may also be concerned about whether students are doing their jobs. Are they working hard enough? Are they spending too much time talking? Is an "off task" student a cause for immediate alarm? Of most concern to teachers may be how much talking students do about a relatively small number of topics. Does the curriculum require students to devote too much time to a single topic, and to topics that are not part of the curriculum for any of their regular school subjects? If the opportunity cost is too high, teachers may feel that they and their students simply have too many other expectations to fulfill. Even if students come to a deep understanding of a topic, there are too many other topics they need to know about.

For that matter, do students even know enough about the kinds of topics proposed as part of our curriculum to be talking about them? Don't students need to first acquire a substantial knowledge base about such subjects, before they can begin to talk meaningfully about them? And aren't there better things for them to spend their time thinking, talking, and writing about? For all these reasons, some teachers may find it harder to feel confident that students are benefitting from these activities, compared to other more familiar kinds of academic work where progress is easier to document. What exactly are students learning?

For these reasons, we believe, it is critical for teachers to have roadmaps of what stands to develop, like those in Chapters 4 and 5, along with new tools for assessing this progress. Still, teachers can overcome doubts and meet the challenges only if they see the value in and are fully committed to developing in students the kinds of intellectual skills that now figure prominently in the new standards and in this book. These skills, as we noted in Chapter 1, are ones that have long been given a favorable nod but that only more recently have assumed center stage and visible commitment.

Committing to the importance of these skills means committing to them not just in principle but also in everyday practice, affording them the time and attention that their importance warrants. Argument and argumentation are core intellectual skills, and they are as real and meaningful as the more familiar, more long-standing objectives of teaching students history or mathematics. These less content-specific skills simply take a different form and arguably require different instructional approaches than do those more content-intensive subjects. In a word, both the objectives and the methods for achieving them may be less familiar to teachers, creating a double challenge to implementation.

Even if a teacher buys in fully to the idea that students should develop skills of argument as core intellectual skills, the question of how best to do it looms large. This is especially so in the absence of well-established, widely accepted metrics like the ones employed to assess reading or mathematics proficiency. This prompts the next question: Is the approach presented in this book the most efficient way to develop these skills? Might there be a more efficient method, one less demanding of students' and teachers' time?

One such method is simple practice. According to the new standards, students should be able to both construct their own arguments and to evaluate arguments critically when they encounter them, most often in written form. Writing and critical reading are of course core literacy skills that have been around for a long time. Literacy objectives continue to be a dominant focus of educators. Why, then, not teach the core skills of critical reading and expository writing directly, perhaps much more efficiently than by means of the dialogic approach we have presented?

In the remainder of this chapter we address this question, as well as the other questions and challenges we have identified. We do so by situating them in a context of what we see as the strengths of the goals and methods advocated in this book. These, we will argue, are sufficient and compelling enough to make the investment and the challenges worth accepting.

Placing Students Front and Center

Reading for a Purpose

Reading and writing are, almost always, solitary activities. Together they define literacy, widely acknowledged as a core objective of education. The Common Core Standards emphasize proficiency in nonfiction reading to a greater extent than has been the case in the past. This shift in emphasis highlights reading to learn, rather than reading as an end in itself, as a key literacy objective.

A harder question is what students need to read and thereby learn about. Here opinions diverge, especially as recommendations become more specific. There may be agreement that some topics are more important than others. But many take the view that the particular topic that a student reads about, especially if the student has chosen it as something he or she is interested in and wants to find out more about, is not what's most important. Rather, it's that the student is exercising and thereby developing the crucial skill of encountering text and extracting meaning from it. Adopting this view takes us from an arena of knowledge acquisition to one of skill development. Students of course need to acquire both, but in this case it is the skill acquisition that makes knowledge acquisition possible. How do we best help students to become proficient in the skill of accessing nonfiction text and extracting knowledge from it?

We propose that this is best done by supporting students in the crucial first step of identifying knowledge that they would like to gain. If they have done this, they then go to the text with a clear purpose. Without such a purpose, students find themselves coping with this common scenario: the teacher instructing them to "read this chapter very carefully because you're going to need to know what's in it for a quiz." Rather than potential gain, the student's only motivation at this point is to avoid future loss (doing poorly on the quiz). Will this prove sufficient to motivate middle-school students to take on and absorb the much greater volume of nonfiction reading that the new standards mandate? There is no reason to think so.

Rather than text or teachers posing questions after the reading, as they do in the traditional scenario, we advocate that instead the questions come first. Furthermore, we suggest that they come from the student rather than from the teacher. Reading for a purpose, and a purpose that is one's own, is the way most adults read most of the time. Shouldn't we, then, give novice readers the same advantage that adults enjoy—of reading for a purpose?

This rationale is reflected in our curriculum. Students read a significant amount of material, but in small doses; and what they read, especially the question-and-answer evidence sets, are read not once but rather reread and reflected on, always within a framework of how they can be used. The primary way that students access information about the topics they are addressing is to pose questions that they think will be useful to them in their argumentation on the topic and then gain access to text excerpts that answer each of these questions. The object is to create in the student a need for the information he or she will acquire. Students will already have an idea of how it will be useful to them because they have posed the questions being asked. The knowledge they gain is knowledge with purpose.

Purposeful knowledge can be contrasted with inert knowledge (Figure 7-1). The latter may be acquired initially but it is immediately stored away in isolation, unconnected to anything else, and most often quickly forgotten. In acquiring purposeful knowledge, in contrast, the learner sees a path to its future use. As a result, he or she has not only the competence but the crucially important *disposition* to use it. In recognizing a purpose for it, the learner values the knowledge that has been acquired and takes ownership of it (Figure 7-2). Competence is necessary, but it is disposition that determines whether competence is used.

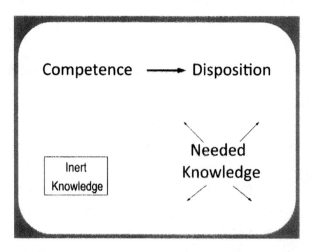

Figure 7-1. Inert vs. purposeful knowledge

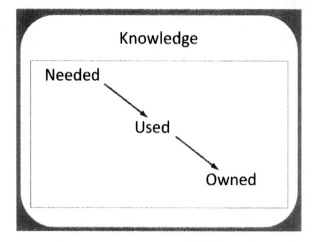

Figure 7-2. Taking ownership of knowledge

Writing to Converse

In implementations of our curriculum, we have found that students do indeed use the knowledge that they gain—both in their electronic dialogs with one another and again in their preparation for and conduct of the final Showdown for the topic. Perhaps the strongest argument for the productivity of the approach comes from the results of the close comparisons between groups of students who participated for multiple years in our curriculum and comparison groups in more traditional classes that emphasized practice in essay writing (see Chapter 6 for details). Despite the greater writing practice gained by these comparison groups, the groups participating in our curriculum outperformed them in outcome measures of individual written argument, as well as dialogic argument, on new topics. Practice alone does not appear to yield the greatest gain in the core literacy objective of expository writing.

The effort to teach argumentive or expository writing has a long and varied history, but very often a disappointing one. Students of all ages find expository writing challenging, and assessments of such writing routinely report this to be the weakest of a student's academic skills at all age levels. This should not be entirely surprising. The multiple contributors to accomplished expository writing make it a skill that challenges all students—and one that most rarely master. Multifaceted by nature, expository writing requires the student to generate ideas that address the topic, develop and articulate each of them into a communicable form, and relate them to one another in ways that form a well-structured whole. The mechanics of expressing them follow. It is not surprising that educators have pointed to cognitive overload as the underlying problem student writers confront.

The demands of producing written text are without doubt significant in their own right, but a possibility is that students find essay writing hard simply because they do not see the point of it. Graff[1] has suggested that too often students see it as an exercise in which one strings together a set of reasonable sounding statements, being careful not to include anything that anyone might challenge. If so, dialogic argumentation becomes a remedy, capable of providing the "missing interlocutor" that gives written argument a point. Conversation has a "naturalness" and, most of all, a purpose that essay writing cannot match. In supplying someone to speak to, and something specific they have said to respond to, dialog greatly reduces production demands.

In turning writing into conversing, our curriculum helps to reduce its formidable demands. The same-side collaboration and opposing-side dialogs that students have engaged in, together with the physical representations of them that they have prepared and can continue to consult, lays a foundation for the interiorized dialog that will become an individual written essay. The "Pre-Write" activity (see appendix supporting materials) is a specific transitional tool that can help students navigate the bridge from conversing to writing.

Purposeful, Student-Directed, Collaborative Engagement and Learning

If the purpose is there, we have suggested, the needed knowledge will follow. This same principle applies to our curriculum even more broadly. From the outset it is structured around a shared purpose and goal. Even though the goal evolves with time, it helps students transition from simply winning to making good arguments.

Two related features are key. First, the curriculum is student-centered, rather than teacher-centered. Students produce the content, in the arguments and counterarguments they generate, in the questions they ask, and in the plans they make with their dialog partners and in their small groups—characteristics not common in most classrooms nor even in many project-based classroom activities. Students take the responsibility of preparing themselves for the final debate, and they work toward that goal. They do this not as an isolated brief assignment, but over a protracted period of time, during which they are always mindful of the final purpose of what they are doing.

Second, the undertaking is shared, or collaborative. Students work with one another toward their joint objectives. Doing so involves listening carefully to one another and responding thoughtfully to what is being said, both by opponents and by same-side peers in pairs and small groups. As we noted in Chapter 1, authentic peer dialog is not common in classrooms. Yet it is common once students exit the classroom door. Hence they are not strangers to it.

Our goal is to capitalize on this familiarity while promoting new norms of "accountable talk" (see Chapter 2).[2] Such talk reflects shared norms regarding acceptable things to say to one another—norms that cannot be imposed from without but must be constructed from within the group and gain acceptance as expected behavior on the part of its members.[3] Claims are expected to have reasons but these reasons must stand to the challenge of strong arguments and evidence that can weaken them. Shared understandings evolve of what acceptable counterarguments consist of and what counts as evidence, and group members risk criticism for violating them.

Collaborative learning has come into fashion these days, but it has not received the serious scrutiny it deserves as a pedagogical practice. It is certainly not the "magic bullet" that will make any learning more effective, if only it is undertaken jointly. The more compelling reason is for students to work together as a group of peers is that it is what will be expected of them in the 21st-century adult society that awaits them. We should be asking and facilitating students to do the kinds of things they will need to do well in that society. Practice is the only way they will gain the needed skill. We have no way to predict exactly what today's students will need to know as adults, but we do know that they will need to learn new skills quickly and well and they will need to work effectively with others in the process. An entirely wrong model of education, we would claim, is one in which students' school years are occupied with activities that we hope will prepare them for totally different kinds of things they will do as adults. Too much of schooling today remains tied to this model—favoring school as preparation, rather than practice, for a future life.

Coaches as Facilitators and Models of Accountable Talk

We have already noted that the role of the teacher in a student-centered curriculum like ours takes some getting used to. It's not easy at first for a teacher to step aside from the customary front-and-center role and let students take over. Having a roadmap of where students are headed, we have suggested, makes it easier, and this is exactly what we wanted to provide in this book. If not the traditional role, then what exactly is the role the teacher should work toward? We have referred to it consistently as the role of coach, but what more precisely does this role look like?

The most important point to emphasize is that in no way does this new role imply that the teacher is an onlooker with nothing to do. To the contrary, the coach's role is an active and exacting one. Because students are taking the lead, this role will be contingent on their behavior and will never be exactly the same from one class to another, or even one day to another. A teacher certainly can't just pull out the lesson plans and expect the class session to unfold exactly as it did the last time.

Nor does this new role imply that the coach never gives direct instructions. In fact, it is probably most accurate to characterize the "coach" role as comprising multiple roles shifting flexibly as circumstances call for, as the video material in Chapter 3 illustrates. Many of the early illustrations are of the coach giving instructions, but the need for instructions diminishes as students become more familiar with the repeating cycle of activities.

The two principal roles a teacher needs to assume and shift between during the course of any class are coach and model. The activities we ask students to engage in and the objectives we ask them to pursue are initially unfamiliar to them. After an initial instruction or later just a reminder, they rarely need to be told *what* to do, but they may need guidance in learning *how* and *why* to do it. Encouragement and approval when productive work is observed is essential and fully as important as suggestions when students don't seem able to self-correct or move in a more productive direction. While students are working in pairs or small groups, a coach cannot be everywhere at once and will not be there every time to make just the right comment to the group needing it. But a coach will be there often enough to keep students moving forward.

The model role is less conspicuous but even more important. By being absorbed and enthusiastic about what students are engaged in doing, and by engaging with them in seeking to fulfill their goals, the teacher is modeling a set of values about what is important and worth doing. This modeling can be more important than anything a teacher could explicitly say to students about what is important. In modeling this engagement, teachers are doing more than telling students to believe in it; they are showing that they themselves believe in it. In a word, they are exhibiting values.

Teachers are powerful modelers of values. They display values all the time in their classrooms, whether they are aware of it or not and whether or not these are values they intend to communicate. Every time they talk about something, and not at all about something else, they display values, conveying implicitly that the first is worth talking about and the second is not. Let us turn then to the topic of values.

From Skills to Values

Developing Shared Norms

We have seen that students participating in our curriculum gradually develop appropriate ways to talk to one another within the context of the shared activities we ask them to engage in. These norms come to be regarded as worthy of upholding and expected of all who would enter the conversation. They are the "ground rules"[4] for participation. Criticism becomes a likely consequence of violations, as we saw in Chapter 5.

These norms, especially at first, are likely to be confined to this special context. Talking to one another outside the classroom, students are likely not to feel the same obligation to give reasons to justify their statements—"That's just how I feel" remains an acceptable explanation to one's peers. Yet we hope that the shared standards of knowing that come to prevail in their argumentation activity will become familiar enough to students that they begin to be aware of them in other contexts as a mode of intellectual discourse, one they come to realize is in fact of wide relevance.

Most notably, they should begin to recognize these standards in their nonfiction reading. They gradually progress beyond the typical student belief in textbooks as revealing unquestioned truth. Rather, they hold authors to a higher standard of justifying their claims with sound arguments and evidence. The claims of those who don't are suspect. Authors are similarly suspect if they don't acknowledge that there exist alternative claims and arguments and address these.

How Do You Know?

Hopefully, the fundamental question "How do you know?" will become a staple of students' thinking in response to all that they read or hear, as well as in what they write. We cannot presume the "How do you know?" stance to be in place and active in any reader or listener. A good deal of research evidence now exists indicating that concepts of knowing evolve with development among children and adolescents.[5,6]

"What does it mean to know something?" is a question that has occupied philosophers for years. At least through their elementary-school years, children hold an *absolutist* understanding of knowledge as an accumulating set of certain facts that are directly apprehended from the external world. Human interpretation and judgment play no role. Their role begins to be recognized with the development of a *relativist* or *multiplist* stance. With it, however, the subjective, human dimension of knowing now takes over. Even reasonable people disagree about significant matters, an adolescent begins to realize. This realization initially assumes such proportions, however, that it may eclipse recognition of any objective standard that could serve as a basis for evaluating conflicting claims. Knowledge now consists not of facts but of opinions, freely chosen by their holders like personal possessions. Everyone can believe what they like, with all opinions accepted as equally right. Knowledge is now seen as emanating from the knower, rather than the known, but at the significant cost of any basis for discriminating among competing knowledge claims.

The next *evaluativist* level of understanding knowing reintegrates the subjective and objective dimensions of knowing. It is a hard-won achievement that not even all adults reach: Even though everyone has a right to their opinion, some opinions are more right than others, to the extent they are supported by reasons and evidence. Knowledge now consists of justified judgments, which require support in a framework of alternatives, evidence, and argument.

Achievement of this evaluativist level of understanding figures critically in coming to value argumentation as a worthwhile undertaking—one that warrants the effort it entails. If knowledge can be attained directly from the external world, as the absolutist maintains, or if knowledge is only unexamined opinion, as the multiplist sees it, there is little incentive to engage in the hard mental work that underlies judgment and evaluation.

We suggest, then, that in engaging in argumentive discourse with peers over a sustained period of time, students are gaining not just cognitive skills and shared behavioral norms, but values. We can refer to these as intellectual values, because they endorse the worth of reasoned discourse. Values are a critical addition to skills. Gaining competence in skills is a necessary condition, but valuing these skills is what determines whether skills will in fact be used beyond the particular context in which they were acquired.

Values are the connecting link between competence and disposition.[6] Only to the extent a young person sees the power and purpose of a way of engaging with the world—sees it value—will he or she become disposed to use it frequently and make it a part of a personal repertory. In the case of argument skills, what do we hope students will come to see as their power? We hope as a more effective means of resolving disagreements than alternatives, certainly, but also as a path to knowing and understanding. Put most simply by one of our young participants near the end of her participation, "Talking about it builds knowledge and your argument for that topic." Another participant told us, "[Discussion] makes you think freely for both sides and agree or disagree with certain points." In the next section, we turn to argumentation as a tool for knowing and for acting in the world. Is it a powerful enough tool that we should regard argumentation as an essential tool for citizenship in a democratic society?

Educating for Citizenship

Given all the other objectives we would like K–12 public education to achieve, ought we be concerned that students come to value argumentive discourse as a mode of relating to one another? One could claim that helping them learn how to get along with one another is a more important objective. Our claim instead would be that developing the skills and values associated with argumentive discourse in fact serves to promote this objective, rather than being at odds with it. Such discourse is the primary means citizens in a democracy have for addressing the matters they jointly face. The premise underlying a democracy is that its citizens possess the skill and disposition to employ these means, to address both smaller and larger issues.

If so, democratic societies are charged with the task of educating their young to fulfill these roles. A democratic society cannot teach its young people what to think; its only feasible mission is to help them learn how to think and to think well. How can they best fulfill this charge? The answer, reflected throughout this book and most explicitly in this chapter, is that young people should engage in the practice of such discourse, from early on and often. There is no better preparation than engaging in the practice itself that we want them to become proficient in. The curriculum presented in this book is founded on this premise.

Collaborative Argumentation

The more specific practice that our curriculum engages students in is debate between two opposing points of view. Not all intellectual discourse takes this form. Collaborative, or coalescent, argumentation,[5] in which two or more participants work together toward solving a problem or achieving a goal, is a common and frequently productive practice. Still, simple argument involving two opposing claims, we believe, is the best initial path to development of collaborative argumentation skills. In oppositional or adversarial argumentation, students learn to listen deeply to one another and to identify and compare contrasting perspectives. These skills they can then take with them to the task of working together in a collaborative mode, where differences must be identified and examined, not smoothed over. Without these skills firmly in place, collaborative argument risks degenerating into an "additive" mode, where successive contributors each add their thoughts but do not address one another directly, and the discussion moves in no particular direction.

Engaging in intellectual discourse gives students not only experience, but with it confidence, in the practice. This skill and confidence they can then apply to any and all of the many kinds of issues, from narrow inter-personal ones to the broad societal ones that they will encounter in a complex modern society. Moreover, they will be able to do so in a range of contexts and with a range of people, from intimates to strangers. And, importantly, they will not hesitate to disagree, because they do not equate challenging ideas with disrespect or intolerance of the individuals holding them.

Acquiring Knowledge as Well as Skills

ZIBELLI

"If you'd argue with me, it would help me decide."

As they engage in such practice, students are acquiring more than just intellectual skills, or even values, that they can apply to new topics. Because they engage deeply with the particular issues they examine, they also come to appreciate and understand these issues as complex ones that do not allow easy resolution. The issues that arise in a democratic society are almost always of this nature. If they were not, they likely would already be resolved.

It does not follow that young people, and even older ones, see them as such. Indeed, it may be difficult for them to take a position at all, as reflected in the adjacent cartoon. This is especially the case if, like the character in the cartoon, they are not accustomed to being listened to. A point of view is indeed likely to be missing to the extent it has never been voiced. And here, as we have claimed throughout the book, lies the power of dialog to develop it, as the cartoon further suggests.

What about the claim that young students lack the knowledge base to engage meaningfully in debate of serious issues? The experience we have gained in implementing our curriculum, as we have reported on it in this book, speaks powerfully against this claim. We ask students to talk about complex matters, and they don't see them as such at the outset. Asked to debate organ sales, for example, many at the outset adopt the stance

"What's the problem? Someone needs a kidney and I want to sell mine. Why not?" Hesitatingly at first, more confidently over time, subtler considerations emerge. Because these are raised in the context of peers voicing criticisms of one another's claims, the issues get the attention they warrant, more than they would if students were simply reading expository text about them (although this too certainly has its place).

When we as their adult guides observe students reasoning in an inadequate, simplistic way about a serious issue like this one, we naturally wonder if we don't need to step in, to make sure the students' thinking doesn't go uncorrected. Often, however, a peer does this quite nicely, as illustrated in the following exchange on the juvenile justice topic.

> A: A child being put in adult prison could save the government a lot of money. Developing educational systems and other parts of a juvenile detention system could cost the government millions of dollars.

> T: So we should put children in adult prison just so we can save money? Juveniles deserve adequate punishments and don't deserve the same thing as adults. Also, if kids aren't put into juvenile systems now, they will end up in it later and adult prisons will become even more crowded . . . juvenile prison is like a first warning and will help keep them out later.

Other times, however, what we observe can be more alarming. To our astonishment, every time we have engaged students in debate on the topic of using animals in research, at least one middle-schooler has expressed the view that a better practice would be to use human prisoners. This is so, they argue, because animals are innocent whereas human prisoners are guilty. The first time we heard this argument, it was not immediately rejected by the arguer's peers and we considered seriously whether we should halt such talk. We have found, however, that a position such as this one does self-correct as students continue to debate, in this case students ultimately getting to the recognition that people are animals too and therefore perhaps deserve the same consideration and protection as nonhuman animals.

Embracing Complexity and Uncertainty

The curriculum sequence we have students engage in for each topic, we have suggested, can be regarded not only as a vehicle for cognitive skill development but also as a model of how to approach a complex issue and to do so in a collaborative manner—generating, examining, reflecting on reasons, coordinating reasons with evidence, and subjecting these lines of reasoning to a reciprocal process of counterargument and rebuttal. It is in this respect that the process is collaborative. At the end of such a process, conceptions of the issue on the part of those arguing both sides are invariably enriched.

Are there general dimensions in terms of which we can conceptualize this enhanced complexity? We propose three:

- **Sophisticated understanding of causality.** Multiple contributors to a complex phenomenon are recognized. Single causes are recognized as inadequate. Causes can be proximal or distal, immediate or delayed.

- **Respect for the role of evidence.** Evidence is treated as fundamental to judging the truth of assertions.

- **Recognition of uncertainty.** Truth doesn't come from authority figures (even presidents, see below) but rather from judgments that are reached through an exacting process of examining alternatives and evidence and reflecting on them.

Each of these dimensions appears in the following dialog between two of our middle-school participants on a highly complex but key civic issue, "Should the USA focus its resources on domestic or international problems?" Key phrases that illustrate these enhanced conceptions appear in bold.

I1: Our country is important but helping the war in Iraq is going to affect us. The point of helping with the War is helping our country.

D1: If we do start focusing first with the problem in Iraq, then what are we supposed to be doing in our country while that is happening? More and more people are suffering here in our country.

I2: But we are wasting $130 Billion per year on that war. It has been $600 Billion since 9/30/08. Don't you think that that is one of the problems that is affecting our economy?

D2: **That's not the only thing** that we are spending money on. But it is one of the biggest that we are spending billions and billions of dollars!

I3: **How do you know for sure** that the budget is one of the biggest? do you know what else we are spending money on, and how much?

D3: We know it must be one of the biggest because when you hear around everywhere "Iraq War" & all this news about people dying in Iraq and etc. etc. We spend almost in total a trillion dollars on that war. It is because of that war that America is in debt.

I4: **But you're saying that you don't know for sure** that the war is the biggest issue affecting our economic crisis. Obama even said in his speech "Our economy is badly weakened, a consequence of greed and irresponsibility on the part of some."

D4: **There you are wrong.** Obama also states that in our main goals we will help other nations.

I5: **no, i am not wrong,** because he doesnt say that the war **caused** the economic crisis. He doesn't say anything directly about causing it.

D5: How can a quote be wrong? look at his speech!

I6: it is his opinion. **Everyone has different opinions on what happens and just because he is the president doesn't mean everything he says is right.**

Teaching the Future

Studying the past is regarded as a foundation for citizenship. Citizens should know how their nation came to be and what it stands for. But the pressures of all that we try to squeeze into the school curriculum are such that the past is studied in lieu of the present, which there ends up being little time for. This is troubling, because it is thinking about the present that affords the practice that students will need to address the problems of tomorrow. Also concerning is the implicit message that this priority of past over present and future conveys to students about what is valued and worth thinking about. We hope this book helps in identifying a potential path to redress this imbalance.

In exploring questions that both interest them and are consequential in the broader society beyond their own families and communities, students gain the opportunity to do what they don't frequently get to do in their classrooms. In so doing they stand to develop a voice of their own, one unafraid to express ideas, to listen to the ideas of others, and to revise their own ideas when warranted. Such voices will carry into the future and serve them well in becoming thinking citizens of a thinking society. We have suggested respects in which our curriculum serves particularly well those young people whose backgrounds and limited opportunities work against their finding such a voice. If engaging them in the kinds of practices we have suggested can move them toward developing such voices, and embracing their roles as citizens of a democracy, no greater purpose can be served.

Notes

1. Graff, G. (2003). *Clueless in academe: How schooling obscures the life of the mind.* New Haven: Yale University Press.

2. Resnick, L.B., Michaels, S., & O'Connor, C. (2010). How (well structured) talk builds the mind. In R. Sternberg & D. Preiss (Eds.), *From genes to context: New discoveries about learning from educational research and their applications.* New York: Springer.

3. Kuhn, D., Zillmer, N., Crowell, A., & Zavala, J. (2013). Developing norms of argumentation: Metacognitive, epistemological, and social dimensions of developing argumentive competence. *Cognition & Instruction, 31 (4)*, 456–496.

4. Mercer, N. (1996). The quality of talk in children's collaborative activity in the classroom. *Learning and Instruction, 6*, 359–377.

5. Moshman, D. (2013). Adolescent rationality. *Advances in Child Development and Behavior*, Vol. 45. Oxford: Elsevier.

6. Kuhn, D. (2009). The importance of learning about knowing. *Perspectives on Child Development, 3*, 112–117.

Appendix 1

· · ·

YEAR ONE

Detailed Curriculum Sequence

I. THE PREGAME: Preparing to encounter our opponents

Based on the opinions expressed in an initial poll on the topic, students are assigned to either a pro or con group for the topic. Until the final Showdown, these groups meet separately.

SESSION 1: GENERATING, SHARING, & THINKING ABOUT REASONS

Materials needed: Large (5"x7") white index cards; paper clips or staplers; copy of topic scenario for each table

Pro and Con Coaches assemble their pro and con groups in separate spaces. Each group divides into teams (A and B, or other names students choose), of 6-8 each, seated around a table, with the 3-4 at each end of table forming a smaller group for some work. For some work, pairs may be formed within the smaller groups. (All time indications are approximate and may need adjustment.)

Coach: Introduce by reiterating (and continuing to emphasize frequently throughout) *what we're doing and why*: **"We want to convince the other side that our position on this issue is the better one and win our final Showdown. This will take some hard work and time to prepare and lots of practice of argument skills."**

Objective: Generating

"Our first task is to be sure we have the best reasons for our position. People can have different reasons for being for or against something. We need to get these reasons out on the table and decide what we think of them."

A. (5 min) *Silent activity.* **"Recall why you chose the position you did. What's your most important reason for being in favor of this position? Write it clearly in large print on a card: '_____ is the better position because _____.' If you have time and a second reason, use a second card."**

Coach: Remind and monitor – only one reason per card.

Objective: Interpreting

B. (5 min) *Small-group activity (3-4 students at either end of table).*

Coach: **"Pass your card to the person on your left. Read & think about the card you receive. If you can't understand it, ask the writer to explain it. Now underneath the reason, REWRITE it using FEWER words. Keep the main point but make it quicker and easier to read later."**

C. (15 min) *Small-group discussion.*

Coach: **"Take turns presenting your 'FEWER-WORDS' VERSION OF YOUR NEIGHBOR'S REASON. One person begins, reading this SHORT VERSION to the group. Does the person who first wrote the reason agree this says it best? Does everyone else understand the reason and agree this is the best way to say it? If not, REWRITE until everyone agrees. CIRCLE the final version or write it on a new card. Put the card in the middle of the table.**

The next person now reads their 'fewer-words' version of their neighbor's reason. REWRITE until everyone understands it & agrees this is the best way to say it.

Now ASK: Is this the SAME reason already in the middle or a different reason?

If it's the same, fasten it to the first reason card, putting the card with the best way to say it on top. If it's different, leave it displayed.

Continue until all reason cards are on the table."

During all group discussions, Coach circulates to facilitate and keep groups on-task, offering mildly supportive comments, e.g., "That reason sounds good." The Coach can suggest candidates for combination, and, if needed for clarity, can propose rewording: "Is there a better way to say this one?" or (if group can't generate) "Would this be better?"

SESSION 1 (CONTINUED)

Objective: Organizing

D. (10-15 min) *Team discussion.* The team COMBINES into one group.

Coach: "Our goal now is to put together the team's reasons into one final set we'll use against our opponents. We need to organize them, getting rid of any duplicates and grouping similar ones together, so we'll have them ready to work for us."

The team can proceed with this task unassisted if able; otherwise Coach provides this structure:

Coach: "1st group, put one of your reasons in the center of table. 2nd group, look carefully at it. Does your group have a similar reason? If it's the same, put your card on top of theirs. If it's similar but saying different things, put it next to the one it's similar to. 1st group, make sure you agree.

2nd group, now put another of your cards out, that has a different reason. 1st group, does your group have a similar reason? If it's the same, put your card on top of theirs. If it's similar but saying different things, put it next to the one it's similar to. 2nd group, make sure you agree. Continue until all cards have been shared.

Now that all cards are in the middle, DOUBLE CHECK. Is each one a different reason? Put the best way to say it on top. Make changes if needed & fasten "same reason" cards together with the best way to say it on top. These are your team's FINAL REASONs."

E. (5 min) *Team discussion.* Each team takes a straw VOTE on which is its strongest reason.

Full-group (2 same-side teams combined) discussion: Each team shares strongest reason with full group.

Coach: **"Are our reasons good enough to win the Showdown?"**

F. (Optional) *Homework.* Each student takes 3 opinion poll sheets home. The assignment: Ask 3 people their position and reason for their position and record it to bring to the next class. *(The sheet is identical to the initial opinion poll students did for their own assignment to pro/con group; it states the issue and asks for a position and justification.)*

Coach: Collect & review, keeping separate, each team's set of final reason cards. Staple duplicates so they don't become detached and work only with top card. Note any that are so unclear or otherwise problematic that they need to be gone over quickly and revised with the team at beginning of next class. For all others, if possible further abbreviate circled reason to fewer words; use a highlighter to highlight the essential words. Highlight briefest possible expression of the reason.

SESSION 2: FINALIZING & EVALUATING REASONS

Materials: More large white index cards and last session's set of final Reason cards for each team

Students assemble in their 6-8 person teams.

A. (5 min) *Silent activity*. Coach distributes Team A's reason cards to Team B and Team B's reason cards to Team A, mentioning that s/he has reviewed them and highlighted the key words.

Coach: "Now you can see the reasons for our position that the other team came up with. See what you think of them."

Teams silently circulate the cards among themselves until everyone has seen them all.

Objective: Adding Reasons

B. (5-10 min) *Team discussion*. Each team receives their OWN CARDS BACK and displays them in center of table.

Coach: "Think about the reasons the other team had – the ones you just looked over. Were there any your team missed?

(If homework was done) **Take out & share the sheets you collected for homework. Look at those from people who had the same-side opinion as ours.** (Save any other-side opinions for later.) **Are there any new ones?"**

Coach: "Now it's time to FINALIZE your team's set of reasons. Are there any you want to add? Remember you want to have the best possible set of reasons to use against your opponents. We want our reasons to hold up against their attacks.

If you want to ADD a reason, put it on a card. Be sure it's not a reason you already have & write it in the clearest, shortest possible way. If everyone agrees, add the card to those on the table. This will be our FINAL SET. Go over it a final time & make any changes."

A desirable goal is at least 6 reasons in final set.

Objective: Evaluating Reasons (INCLUDE C ONLY FOR INITIAL 1-2 TOPIC CYCLES; THEN OMIT)

C. (5 min) *Optional full-group discussion. (This can be done either within same-side groups or as a whole-class activity.)* Students are asked how they know their reasons are good ones. (How did they choose their "best" reason last session?) This leads to a discussion of what makes a reason a good one and to the idea that reasons may be of different quality.

Coach: "Are some reasons really better than other reasons? Or is any reason just as good as any other reason?"

Coaches don't try to dissuade those who subscribe to the all-equal view, but ask for ideas about what might make one reason better than another. Coach can conclude the discussion by summarizing a few possible criteria for a reason being a good one, e.g., maybe a good reason would be better convincing people who disagree than would a not-so-good reason. Or: A good reason might have good evidence to support it.

SESSION 2 (CONTINUED)

Objective: Evaluating Reasons (continued)

D. (10-15 min) *Small-group discussion.*

Coach: "Let's agree which are our stronger reasons, the ones that will do the most work for us. Talk it over & agree WHY a reason belongs in a category before you put it there."

Each small group takes HALF of their team's reason CARDS. Students are asked to SORT reason cards into 3 piles – BEST, OKAY, SO-SO (or students choose their own category names).

Three folded ("tent") cards should be prepared with BEST, OKAY or SO-SO displayed on them, as markers for the 3 piles.

Coaches can be flexible as to when to transition from D to E, allowing students to move to E as soon as they seem ready.

Value of this activity depends on keeping the focus on "reasons for reasons," i.e., on WHY a particular reason belongs in that category. For the first few times doing this activity, Coaches can suggest they focus on the top and bottom ends and use the middle category for ones they're not sure of or maybe want to come back to, or can't agree on.

E. (10-15 min) *Team discussion.* Small groups reassemble into their team. Each small group displays on table center the reason cards in their BEST pile.

Coach: "Now you need to persuade the other half of your team that the reasons in your BEST pile really belong there. If they disagree, try to persuade your teammates with a REASON why the reason is a good one ("Reasons for Reasons"). Take turns doing this for each of your BEST reasons, until the whole team agrees which reasons are going to be in the team's final set of BEST reasons. These are the ones that are going to do the work for us against our opponents."

At Coach's discretion, Okay- as well as Best-category Reason cards can be included in final set. Optimum total number is 4-6 cards in Best or Best/Okay category.

F. (3 min) *Same-side full-group discussion.* Coach solicits from each team what they have decided is their best reason. May repeat for 2nd-best reason.

G. (5 min) (If no time, postpone to beginning of next session.) *Full-group discussion.*

Coach: "So, how good are our reasons are at this point? Good enough to win?? (Elicit response.) But remember that while we've been doing this, the other side has been coming up with their reasons for having the opposite position on this issue. Soon you're going to hear their reasons! To win the Showdown, we're going to have to pay attention to their reasons too. What do you think some of their reasons might be?" (If any other-side reasons were obtained as homework, these can now be used as a source.)

Coaches don't formally encourage (but don't discourage if it happens spontaneously) generating counterarguments to the other-side reasons that are volunteered. Encourage students to remember them for later: "They'll be very important."

Coach may make concluding comment: **"I wonder if we're right - that these ARE their reasons. We'll find out soon."**

Coach: Collect each team's final set of Reason cards, separated into the 3 category piles, fastened & labeled, & keep them accessible to student for reference throughout Phases II & III.

II. THE GAME: Electronic dialogs

MIDDLE SESSIONS: PAIR DIALOGS

The next sessions are devoted to a series of electronic dialogs that a student and same-side partner conduct with a series of pairs from the opposing side.

Materials: One computer per student pair, w/ appropriate software & connectivity. (Fallback in case of equipment lack or breakdown: Opposing pairs can pass a laptop or writing pad back and forth to conduct the dialog.) Coach prepares a roster pairing each pair to a different opposing pair for each session. Reason cards from Pregame sessions should be available for reference; blank Reflection sheets (see Supplementary Materials for samples).

A. Introduction to dialogs (1st session only)

Coach: **"Now it's time to hear what your opponents have to say and start working to defeat them. Are you ready to confront them??"** (Elicit some student reactions.)

Two points bear emphasis at this session (and thereafter as needed):

- **Work TOGETHER to decide what to say.** (Two heads are better than one!) Give positive & negative examples of what working together means. It does not mean dividing up the work (e.g., you think what to say and I'll type). It does mean talking to one another and working out any disagreement you have before you type.

- Think carefully about what your opponents have said & **RESPOND** to it directly; try to respond to their claim; don't just ignore it because you think your point is better.

B. Dialogs (1st session & continuing)

Students sit with assigned same-side partner, connect to software and wait for the opposing pair assigned for that day to do same. One pair is assigned to initiate the dialog.

Coach: **"While you're waiting for a response, you can discuss with one another how you think the opponents are going to respond and what would be best to say in return. In other words, PLAN your strategy. You'll also have a REFLECTION SHEET to work on while you're waiting."**

*Optional, if needed to help pair focus: Pair can also complete a **Prediction Sheet**, recording what they predict opponent will say (see Supplementary Materials).*

C. Reflection Sheets

These are presented at each dialog session, one each session per same-side pair. Distribute once dialogs are well underway – about 10 min into session – & reserve last 10 min of session to complete them.

Coach: **"These sheets will help you think about & have a record of today's work, to use in the Showdown"** (at initial distribution & repeated as necessary thereafter).

Reflection sheets are of two types alternated across sessions (see Supplementary Materials for samples). Focus of the "**Other**" sheet is: What is one of their main arguments and what was our response (counterargument)? Was there a better counterargument to use? Focus of the "**Own**" sheet is: What is one of our main arguments and what was their counterargument and our Comeback (rebuttal)? Was there a better Comeback we could have used?

At 1st session distribute Other sheet, at 2nd session Own sheet, & alternate thereafter. If students are capable & finish before others, they can be given alternate sheet to also do.

At each session, pairs are told who new opponent pair will be & agenda is repeated.

Coach: Collect & save reflection sheets for later use.

FINAL (4ᵀᴴ) TOPIC CYCLE:

D. Near the beginning of the 1ˢᵗ dialog session for this topic, introduce casually the topic evidence that will play a more formal role in Year 2.

Coach: **"This time we have some EVIDENCE available you may want to use to strengthen your arguments. A set of sheets with a QUESTION on each (and ANSWER inside) about our topic is here for your use."**

Evidence set consists of 8x11" sheets, each with a relevant question printed on one side and the sheet folded to conceal the answer printed inside (see Supplementary Materials for sample). One set remains nearby for each team's use.

ONCE during each dialog session, remind students that evidence is available.

Coach: **"Remember the Evidence Questions & Answers are here for your use if you think they will help you."**

III. THE ENDGAME: Showdown prep, Showdown, and Debrief

Showdown Preparation: 2 sessions

SESSION 1: PREPARING TO COUNTER OTHERS' REASONS

Materials needed: All completed "Other" Reflection sheets. Blank PINK (or other pastel color) "Other" Reflection sheets; paper-clips

Students reassemble in their original teams.

The goal of this session is for teams to produce a final set of "Other" Reflection sheets, for reference during the Showdown. By session end, teams should have one final (pink) "Other" sheet for **each** of the other side's reasons. It should contain the team's best Counter to that reason.

Coach: "We'll want to know all the others' arguments and have our best counterarguments to them at our fingertips during the Showdown. Getting them ready is our task for today."

Objective: Organizing Other-side Reasons

A. (10 min) *Team activity.* All of the "**Other**" Reflection sheets that have been produced are divided & distributed, half to each team.

Coach: "Your task is to sort these into piles, with one pile for each different OTHER-SIDE reason. So read their reasons & put all those that are the same reason in one pile."

The team may further divide the sheets and break into small groups for this task, but then reassemble to integrate their piles, so the team produces only one pile for each Other-side reason.

B. (5 min) *Team activity.* Once team is finished, Coach prompts them to review:

"Are you sure you have just one pile for each different reason? Double-check."

Coach: "Are there any Other-side reasons you've heard in your dialogs (or from reasons you've heard from others outside class) that are missing?" An additional Reflection sheet can be created for any such reason.

Objective: Finalizing Counters to Other-side Reasons

C. (15 min) *Pair discussion.* The Coach provides blank PINK (or other pastel color) SUMMARY REFLECTION SHEETS & instructs students to place one on top of each pile & paper-clip pile.

Teams assemble into PAIRS & each pair takes a share of the piles.

Coach: "Your task now is to examine each pile, one at a time, review our Counters to this reason that are written on the sheets, & decide on the single BEST COUNTER. Write a FEWEST-WORDs version of the Other-side reason & its Best Counter on the FINAL (pink) Reflection sheet, so you'll have it ready for the Showdown."

D. (10 min) *Pair discussion.*

Coach: "Exchange your piles, with pink sheets on top, with another pair. Review the other pair's work. Have your teammates written on the pink sheet the best, strongest COUNTER, the one that will do the most damage to this reason? Is there a better Counter or a better way to say this one? If so, make suggestions to the other pair."

Exchanges across pairs can be continued as time permits.

E. (5 min) *Team discussion.* The team reviews the full set of pink sheets & agrees on the final set, each containing an **Other-side reason** & its **Best possible counter** to other-side reasons, to be used in the Showdown.

F. (5 min) *Optional same-side full-group discussion.* Coach solicits responses from entire group: "**What's their toughest reason for us to counter? How will we counter it?**"

Coach: Separate each top pink sheet from pile and save each team's set for Showdown. Keep separate the sets of pink sheets from different teams.

SESSION 2: PREPARING TO REBUT OTHERS' COUNTERS TO OUR REASONS (COMEBACKS)

Materials needed: All completed "Own" Reflection sheets. Blank green (or other pastel color) "Own" Reflection sheets; paper-clips

The goal of this session is for teams to produce a final set of "Own" Reflection sheets. By session end, teams should have one final (green) "Own" sheet for **each** of the team's own-side reasons. It should contain the Other side's most likely counters & the team's best Rebuttal to each.

Coach: "We'll need to have one of these sheets for each of our reasons at our fingertips during the Showdown, so we know what to come back with when they try to attack our reasons. Getting them ready is our task for today."

Objective: Organizing Own-side Reasons

A. (7-10 min) *Team activity*. All of the "**Own**" Reflection sheets that have been produced are divided & distributed, half to each team.

Coach: "Sort these into piles, with one pile for each of our reasons (like the cards we made earlier)."

The team may further divide the sheets and break into small groups for this task, but then reassemble to integrate their piles, so the team produces only one pile for each Own-side reason.

B. (3 min) *Team activity*. Once team is finished, Coach prompts them to review.

Coach: "Are you sure you have just one pile for each different reason? Double-check."

Objective: Organizing Counters to Own-side Reasons

C. (10 min) *Pair discussion*. The Coach provides blank GREEN SUMMARY REFLECTION SHEETS & instructs students to place one on top of each pile & paper-clip pile.

Teams assemble into PAIRS & each pair takes a share of the piles.

Coach: "Examine each pile, one at a time, review the Counters to our reason that are written on the sheets, & bring to the top of the pile the 1-3 sheets showing the toughest, most damaging Counters to our reason. There may be only one good Counter; there could be 2 or 3. Write a FEWEST-WORDs version of each of these Counters on the green sheet."

Objective: Finalizing Rebuttals

D. (10 min) *Pair discussion*.

Coach: "Now your final step. For each green sheet, look through the old sheets & find our best COMEBACK (Rebuttal) to that Counter to our reason. Write it on the green sheet below the Counter, to have ready for the Showdown."

E. (10 min) *Pair discussion*.

Coach: "Exchange your piles, with green sheets on top, with another pair. Review the other pair's work. Have your teammates written on the green sheet the best, strongest Comeback to each Counter, the one that will best save our reason? Is there a better Comeback or a better way to say this one? If so, make suggestions to the other pair."

Exchanges across pairs can be continued as time permits.

F. (3-5 min) *Team discussion*. The team reviews the full set of green sheets & agrees on the final set.

G. (5 min) *Optional same-side full-group discussion*. Coach solicits responses from entire group: "**What's their toughest counter for us to rebut? How will we do it?**"

Coach: *Separate green sheets from piles and save for team's use in Showdown.*

Showdown: 1 session

Materials needed: stopwatch; previous materials prepared by students; audio or video recording device

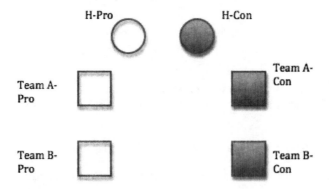

Pro & Con teams assemble together, seated on opposite sides of the room. The A & B teams within each toss a coin (or Coach assigns) which one will be in charge first. A coin toss determines whether Pro or Con team speaks first. The team not in charge sits behind the active group and observes and may pass notes to the team in charge but are otherwise silent. Individual chairs for the two Hotseat speakers are placed at the front of the room, facing one another. Coach reviews Showdown rules. (See Supplementary Materials.) Colored summary reflection sheets from previous sessions are distributed to each team (and other earlier materials made accessible), and the teams are offered an initial 5-10-min "huddle" to get organized and decide their strategy and a tentative order of speakers.

Debrief: 1 session

Materials needed: video viewing equipment if students are to be shown a recording of part of the showdown; copies of a transcription of selected portions of the showdown

Begin the session with 10 min of silent review of the **Argument Map** (one side's statements appearing in the left column and the other side's in the right) segment that has been distributed. Beginning students at first won't be ready to do so, but by the end of year 1 students should be able to make judgments regarding the merit of each argument move and make penciled notations of these. Coach then leads students through a discussion of why each statement was scored the way it was by the adults who did the scoring. Students can object to a particular scoring, with others invited to respond, as long as this discussion remains productive. A student who remains dissatisfied can be invited to submit a written argument for consideration by an expert judge who will make the final scoring decision.

Potential talking points and scoring:

1. Did a statement **ignore** what the opponent had just said to introduce a new idea? (0 points)

2. Did a statement **counter** what the opponent had said in a way that **weakened** it? (1 point)

3. Did a response to a counter (rebuttal) restore strength to the speaker's point? (1 point)

4. Did the speaker make an **unwarranted assumption**? (minus 1 point)

5. If **evidence** was cited, was it used in the **service** of an argument (not just cited)? (1 point)

   (Evidence cited but not used can be awarded ½ point.)

At the end of the session, coaches announce as a winner the side having the larger number of points based on their scoring of the showdown. Students can be advised to consult individually outside of class regarding the scoring of any particular segment that was not covered during the class debrief.

Final essay: 1 session or as a homework assignment

In a final individual essay assignment, students may take either the pro or con position, regardless of the side they took during the activity.

In an optional "Pre-write" activity, students are instructed to "have an argument with yourself." The student divides a sheet of paper in half lengthwise and begins by writing their own position and justification for it in the left column. In the right column they write "what another person who disagreed might say" and then in the left column what they might say in return. From 6-10 entries in each column should be completed. This document then becomes a resource for writing the final essay. (See Supplementary materials.) The first time this assignment is given, the Coach may present a verbal/physical illustration, playing both roles by moving between two chairs to depict each of the positions.

Appendix 2

■ ■ ■

YEAR TWO

Detailed Curriculum Sequence

I. THE PREGAME: Preparing to encounter our opponents

Based on the opinions expressed in an initial poll on the topic, students are assigned to either a pro or con group for the topic. Until the final Showdown, these groups meet separately.

SESSION 1: GENERATING, SHARING, & THINKING ABOUT REASONS (OPTIONAL)

Materials needed: Large (5"x7") white index cards; paper clips or staplers; copy of topic scenario for each table; homework sheets if used; Small (3"x3") yellow post-its; small (3"x5") yellow index cards

Pro and Con Coaches assemble their pro and con groups in separate spaces. Each group divides into teams (A and B, or other names students choose), of 6-8 each, seated around a table, with the 3-4 at each end of table forming a smaller group for some work. For some work, pairs may be formed within the smaller groups. (All time indications are approximate and may need adjustment.)

Coach: Introduce by reiterating (and continuing to emphasize frequently throughout) *what we're doing and why*: **"We want to convince the other side that our position on this issue is the better one and win our final Showdown. This will take some hard work and time to prepare and lots of practice of argument skills."**

Objective: Generating

"Our first task is to be sure we have the best reasons for our position. We need to get these reasons out on the table and decide what we think of them."

A. (5 min) *Silent activity.* **"Recall why you chose the position you did. What's your most important reason for being in favor of this position? Write it clearly in large print on a card: '_____ is the better position because _____.' If you have time and a second reason, use a second card."**

Coach: Remind and monitor – only one reason per card.

Objective: Interpreting

B. (5 min) *Small-group activity (3-4 students at either end of table).*

Coach: **"Pass your card to the person on your left. Read & think about the card you receive. If you can't understand it, ask the writer to explain it. Now underneath the reason, REWRITE it using FEWER words. Keep the main point but make it quicker and easier to read later."**

C. (15 min) *Small-group discussion.*

Coach: **"Take turns presenting your 'FEWER-WORDS' VERSION OF YOUR NEIGHBOR'S REASON. One person begins, reading this SHORT VERSION to the group. Does the person who first wrote the reason agree this says it best? Does everyone else understand the reason and agree this is the best way to say it? If not, REWRITE until everyone agrees. CIRCLE the final version or write it on a new card. Put the card in the middle of the table.**

The next person now reads their 'fewer-words' version of their neighbor's reason. REWRITE until everyone understands it & agrees this is the best way to say it.

Now ASK: Is this the SAME reason already in the middle or a different reason?

If it's the same, fasten it to the first reason card, putting the card with the best way to say it on top. If it's different, leave it displayed.

Continue until all reason cards are on the table."

During all group discussions, the Coach circulates to facilitate and keep groups on-task, offering mildly supportive comments, e.g., "That reason sounds good." The Coach can suggest candidates for combination, and, if needed for clarity, can propose rewording: "Is there a better way to say this one?" or (if group can't generate) "Would this be better?"

SESSION 1 (CONTINUED)

Objective: Organizing

D. (10-15 min) *Team discussion*. The team COMBINES into one group.

Coach: "Our goal now is to put together the team's reasons into one final set we'll use against our opponents. We need to organize them, getting rid of any duplicates and grouping similar ones together, so we'll have them ready to work for us."

The team can proceed with this task unassisted if able; otherwise Coach provides this structure:

Coach: "1st group, put one of your reasons in the center of table. 2nd group, look carefully at it. Does your group have a similar reason? If it's the same, put your card on top of theirs. If it's similar but saying different things, put it next to the one it's similar to. 1st group, make sure you agree.

2nd group, now put another of your cards out, that has a different reason. 1st group, does your group have a similar reason? If it's the same, put your card on top of theirs. If it's similar but saying different things, put it next to the one it's similar to. 2nd group, make sure you agree. Continue until all cards have been shared.

Now that all cards are in the middle, DOUBLE CHECK. Is each one a different reason? Put the best way to say it on top. Make changes if needed & fasten "same reason" cards together with the best way to say it on top. These are your team's FINAL REASONs."

E. (5 min) *Team discussion*. Each team takes a straw VOTE on which is its strongest reason.

Full-group (2 teams combined) discussion: Each team shares strongest reason with full group.

Coach: "Are our reasons good enough to win the Showdown?"

F. (Optional) *Homework*. Each student takes 3 opinion poll sheets home. The assignment: Ask 3 people their position and reason for their position and record it to bring to the next class. *(The sheet is identical to the initial opinion poll students did for their own assignment to pro/con group; it states the issue and asks for a position and justification.)*

Coach: Collect & review, keeping separate, each team's set of final reason cards. Staple duplicates so they don't become detached and work only with top card. Note any that are so unclear or otherwise problematic that they need to be gone over quickly and revised with team at beginning of next class. For all others, if possible further abbreviate circled reason to fewer words; use a highlighter to highlight the essential words. Highlight briefest possible expression of the reason.

SESSION 2: FINALIZING REASONS; ATTACHING EVIDENCE

*Materials: More large white index cards; last session's set of final **Reason cards** for each team; small (3"x3") **yellow post-its**; small (3"x5") **yellow index cards**; duplicate **Evidence sets** for each team (4 sets total)*

Students assemble in their 6-8 person teams.

A. (5 min) *Silent activity.* Coach distributes Team A's reason cards to Team B and Team B's reason cards to Team A, mentioning that s/he has reviewed them and highlighted the key words.

Coach: "Now you can see the reasons for our position that the other team came up with. See what you think of them."

Teams silently circulate the cards among themselves until everyone has seen them all.

Objective: Adding Reasons

B. (5 min) *Team discussion.* Each team receives their OWN CARDS BACK and displays them in center of table.

Coach: "Think about the reasons the other team had – the ones you just looked over. Were there any your team missed?

(If homework was done) **Take out & share the sheets you collected for homework. Look at those from people who had the same-side opinion as ours.** (Save any other-side opinions for later.) **Are there any new ones?"**

Coach: "Now it's time to FINALIZE your team's set of reasons. Are there any you want to add? Remember you want to have the best possible set of reasons to use against your opponents. We want our reasons to hold up against their attacks.

If you want to ADD a reason, put it on a card. Be sure it's not a reason you already have & write it in the clearest, shortest possible way. If everyone agrees, add the card to the set on the table." This will be our FINAL SET. Go over it a final time & make any changes."

A desirable goal is at least 6 reasons in final set.

C. (2 min) *Full-group discussion.*

Coach: "How do our reasons look for this topic? Are they strong? Are the opponents going to be able to counter them? Are we going to be able to rebut their counters? Today we'll find out how strong they are by seeing what evidence there is to attach to them"

Objective: Introducing Evidence (INCLUDE D ONLY FOR INITIAL TOPIC CYCLE; THEN OMIT)

D. (3 min) *Full-group discussion.*

Coach: "This year we're going to work on using EVIDENCE (of the sort we introduced last year) to strengthen our arguments.

(How) Will evidence make any of our reasons stronger? Will it make it harder for opponents to counter them?

To save the time of your having to search yourselves, we have answers to some of the factual questions you might have. A set of sheets with a QUESTION on each (and ANSWER inside) about our topic is here for your use."

Coach reviews procedures for access to these.

SESSION 2 (CONTINUED)

Objective: Attaching Evidence

E. (15 min) *Small-group or pair activity.* Each team DIVIDES into small groups & divides the team's set of REASON cards among them. The coach distributes an identical set of EVIDENCE to each small group (2 sets for each team). (Depending on group size, the group may further divide into pairs.)

Coach: "With your partner(s), look at the Reason card(s) you are responsible for and ask yourselves, 'Could the answers to any of these Evidence questions help support this reason?' If so, get the answer & use a YELLOW POST-IT to write a one-sentence summary of it. ATTACH the post-it to the Reason card. Do the same for each Reason card."

Coach: Have multiple evidence sets prepared, two sets per team (i.e., one per group or 2 pairs).

Depending on students' capability, the number of pieces of evidence introduced at Session 2 may be gradually increased over subsequent topics.

Depending on students' capability, the following addition may be introduced now or delayed until later.

Coach: "While you're doing this, new questions you'd like answers to may occur to you. If so, write the question on a YELLOW EVIDENCE CARD and turn it in today; we'll try to get answers for you."

For the next session, coaches find brief answers to these & a Q&A sheet for each is added to the Evidence set.

A reminder of this opportunity should be given at the beginning of each session from this point on (through each Dialog and Showdown Prep session).

F. (10 min) *Small-group discussion.*

Coach: "Exchange the Reason card(s) you worked on with another group. Taking turns, explain to them which piece(s) of evidence, if any, helps support this Reason and HOW it does. If they agree, leave the post-it fastened to the Reason card it supports. If not, make corrections. If the reviewing group sees opportunities to use evidence that the first group missed, they can suggest and add them."

If time, F. can be repeated across different groups.

Coach: "A Reason card may have MORE THAN ONE PIECE OF EVIDENCE attached to it. Also, one piece of Evidence may support MORE THAN ONE REASON; in this case you'll need to attach another post-it of it to the other Reason card it supports."

Coach: Collect, & keep separate by team, Reason cards with Evidence to return at beginning of next session.

SESSION 3: ATTACHING EVIDENCE & FINALIZING REASONS WITH EVIDENCE (OPTIONAL)

*Materials needed: Small (3"x3") **yellow post-its**; small (3"x5") **yellow index cards**; each small group's share of **Reason** cards & **Evidence** from last session*

Objective: Attaching Evidence (continued)

A. (15 min) *Small-group or pair activity*. This activity repeats E & F from Session 2, with new pieces of evidence (about 6) added to the original set. Each team DIVIDES into small groups & divides REASON cards among pairs. (Groups should take different Reason cards than those they had in Session 2.) The coach distributes an identical set of EVIDENCE (old & new) to each small group (2 sets for each team).

Coach: "Look at the Reason card(s) your group is responsible for and ask yourselves, 'Could the answers to any of the Evidence questions help support this reason?' If so, get the answer & use a YELLOW POST-IT to write a one-sentence summary of it and ATTACH the post-it to the Reason card, along with any other Evidence post-its that are already there from last session. Do the same for each Reason card."

Coach: Have multiple evidence sets prepared, two sets per team.

Depending on students' capability, the following addition may be introduced or delayed.

Coach: "While you're doing this, new questions you'd like answers to may occur to you. If so, write the question on a YELLOW EVIDENCE CARD and turn it in today; we'll try to get answers for you."

For the next session, coaches seek answers to these & the questions & answers are added to the Evidence set.

A reminder of this opportunity should be given at the beginning of each session from this point on (through each Dialog and Showdown Prep session).

B. (10 min) *Small-group discussion.*

Coach: "Exchange the Reason card(s) you worked on with another group. Explain which piece(s) of evidence, if any, helps support this Reason and HOW it does. If they agree, leave the post-it fastened to the Reason card it supports. If not, make corrections. If time, exchange with another group."

Coach reminds: "A Reason card may have MORE THAN ONE PIECE OF EVIDENCE attached to it. Also, one piece of Evidence may support MORE THAN ONE REASON."

SESSION 3 (CONTINUED)

Objective: Finalizing Reasons with Evidence

C. (10 min) *Team discussion.* Team displays for review its total set of Reason cards with Evidence post-its.

Coach: "Circulate your completed Reason cards around the table to make sure everyone has seen them all. This is the final set of Reasons with Evidence that you're going to take into battle with your opponents. (Could an opponent challenge you, saying, "That's not evidence for your reason.") Look over everything carefully & make sure you're satisfied.

When you're finished, also look over the Evidence set . Is there any evidence you haven't made use of? Is there any way that evidence can help you?"

D. (Optional, if time) (10 min) *Team discussion.* Teams exchange Reason cards & review one another's work.

Teams also assemble any yellow index cards containing **NEW Evidence questions** & submit these to Coach.

Coach may if warranted impose a maximum on these and ask team to submit their most important 4. If team is generating many questions without difficulty, coach may also request that the team indicate on the back of the card why and how an answer will be useful to them: "What will the answer to this question show?"

Coach examines submitted questions and at this or the next session returns to the writers for clarification any questions that are not clear or precise enough to allow informative answers. For the next session, coaches secure answers & add the Q&A pair to the evidence set.

E. (5 min) *Full-group discussion.*

Coach: "So, how good are you thinking our reasons are at this point? Good enough to win?? (Elicit response.) But remember that while we've been doing this, the other side has been coming up with their reasons for having the opposite position on this issue. Soon you're going to hear their reasons! You know by now to win the Showdown, we're going to have to pay attention to their reasons too. What do you think some of their reasons might be?" (If any other-side reasons were obtained as homework, these can now be used as a source.)

Coaches don't formally encourage (but don't discourage if it happens spontaneously) generating counterarguments to the other-side reasons that are volunteered. Students are encouraged to remember them for later: "They'll be very important."

Coach may make concluding comment: **"I wonder if we're right - that these ARE their reasons. We'll find out soon."**

Coach: Collect each team's final set of Reason cards, with Evidence post-its attached, & keep them accessible for reference throughout Phases II & III.

II. THE GAME: Electronic dialogs

The next sessions are devoted to a series of electronic dialogs that a student and same-side partner conduct with a series of pairs from the opposing side.

Materials: One computer per student pair, w/ appropriate software & connectivity. (Fallback in case of equipment lack or breakdown: Opposing pairs can pass a laptop or writing pad back and forth to conduct the dialog.) Coach prepares a roster pairing each pair to a different opposing pair for each session. Reason cards from Pregame sessions; duplicate Evidence sets (one per team) should be available for reference; blank Reflection sheets (see Supplementary Materials for samples); small (3"x3") yellow post-its; small (3"x5") yellow index cards; optional: for each team, a sheet listing all Evidence questions (useful when Evidence sets become large).

A. Introduction to dialogs (1ˢᵗ session only)

Coach: **"Now it's time to hear what your opponents have to say and start working to defeat them. Are you ready to confront them??"** (Elicit some student reactions.)

Two points bear emphasis at this session (and thereafter as needed):

- **Work TOGETHER to decide what to say** (Two heads are better than one!) Give positive & negative examples of what working together means. It does not mean dividing up the work (e.g., you think what to say and I'll type). It does mean talking to one another and working out any disagreement you have before you type.

- Think carefully about what your opponents have said & **RESPOND** to it directly; try to weaken their claim; don't just ignore it because you think your point is better.

B. Dialogs (1ˢᵗ session & continuing)

Students sit with assigned same-side partner, connect to software and wait for the opposing pair assigned for that day to do same. One pair is assigned to initiate the dialog.

Coach: **"While you're waiting for a response, you can discuss with one another how you think the opponents are going to respond and what would be best to say in return. In other words, PLAN your strategy. You'll also have a REFLECTION SHEET to work on while you're waiting."**

*Optional, if needed to help pair focus: Pair can also complete a **Prediction Sheet**, recording what they predict opponent will say (see Supplementary Materials).*

C. Reflection Sheets

These are presented at each dialog session, one each session per same-side pair. Distribute once dialogs are well underway – about 10 min into session – & reserve last 10 min of session to complete them.

Coach: **"These sheets will help you think about & have a record of today's work, to use in the Showdown"** (at initial distribution & repeated as necessary thereafter).

Reflection sheets are of two types alternated across sessions (see Supplementary Materials for samples). Focus of the "**Other**" sheet is: What is one of their main arguments and what was our response (counterargument)? Was there a better counterargument to use? Focus of the "**Own**" sheet is: What is one of our main arguments and what was their counterargument and our Comeback (rebuttal)? Was there a better Comeback we could have used?

At 1st session distribute Other sheet, at 2nd session Own sheet, & alternate thereafter. If students are capable & finish before others, they can be given alternate sheet to also do.

Year 2 Reflection sheets contain space for Evidence Post-its (see Supplementary Materials).

Coach: **"On your Reflection sheets, you'll want to include your most important EVIDENCE, so it's handy. Either rewrite a post-it to attach or move it from a Reason card. A Reflection sheet isn't really finished until it has some evidence on it.**

Also remember, new questions you'd like answers to may occur to you. If so, write the question on a YELLOW EVIDENCE CARD and turn it in; we'll try to get answers for you."

For the next session, coaches seek answers to these & the questions & answers are added to the Evidence set.

At the next dialog session, pairs are told who new opponent pair will be & agenda is repeated.

Coach: Collect & save reflection sheets for later use.

III. THE ENDGAME: Showdown prep, Showdown, and Debrief

Showdown Preparation: 2 sessions

SESSION 1: PREPARING TO COUNTER OTHERS' REASONS

Materials needed: All completed "Other" Reflection sheets. Blank PINK (or other pastel color) "Other" Reflection sheets; paper-clips. Small (3"x3")yellow post-its; small (3"x5") yellow index cards

Students reassemble in their original teams.

The goal of this session is for teams to produce a final set of "Other" Reflection sheets, for reference during the Showdown. By session end, teams should have one final (pink) "Other" sheet for **each** of the other side's reasons. It should contain the team's best Counter to that reason.

Coach: **"We'll want to know all the others' arguments and have our best counterarguments to them at our fingertips during the Showdown. Getting them ready is our task for today."**

Objective: Organizing Other-side Reasons

A. (10 min) *Team activity.* All of the "**Other**" Reflection sheets that have been produced are divided & distributed, half to each team.

Coach: **"Your task is to sort these into piles, with one pile for each different OTHER-SIDE reason. So read their reasons & put all those that are the same reason in one pile."**

The team may further divide the sheets and break into small groups for this task, but then reassemble to integrate their piles, so the team produces only one pile for each Other-side reason.

B. (5 min) *Team activity.* Once team is finished, Coach prompts them to review: **"Are you sure you have just one pile for each different reason? Double-check."**

Coach: **"Are there any Other-side reasons you've heard in your dialogs (or from reasons you've heard from others outside class) that are missing?"** An additional Reflection sheet can be created for any such reason.

Objective: Finalizing Counters to Other-side Reasons

C. (15 min) *Pair discussion.* The Coach provides blank PINK SUMMARY REFLECTION SHEETS & instructs students to place one on top of each pile & paper-clip pile.

Teams assemble into PAIRS & each pair takes a share of the piles.

Coach: **"Your task now is to examine each pile, one at a time, review our Counters to this reason that are written on the sheets, & decide on the single BEST COUNTER. Write a FEWEST-WORDS version of the Other-side reason & its Best Counter on the FINAL (pink) Reflection sheet, so you'll have it ready for the Showdown.**

Move any helpful yellow EVIDENCE post-its to the Final pink sheet. Make a new post-it for any new evidence you now have."

D. (10 min) *Pair discussion.*

Coach: **"Exchange your piles, with pink sheets on top, with another pair. Review the other pair's work. Have your teammates written on the pink sheet the best, strongest COUNTER, the one that will do the most damage to this reason? Is there a better Counter or a better way to say this one? If so, make suggestions to the other pair."**

Exchanges across pairs can be continued as time permits. Suggestions by one pair to another can be made verbally or by (a new color) post-it.

E. (5 min) *Team discussion.* The team reviews the full set of pink sheets & agrees on the final set, containing an **Other-side reason** & its **Best possible counter** to other-side reasons, to be used in the Showdown.

F. (5 min) *Optional full-group discussion.* Coach solicits responses from entire group: **"What's their toughest reason for us to counter? How will we counter it?"**

Coach: *Separate each top pink sheet from pile and save each team's set for Showdown. Keep separate the sets of pink sheets from different teams.*

SESSION 2: PREPARING TO REBUT OTHERS' COUNTERS TO OUR REASONS (COMEBACKS)

Materials needed: All completed "Own" Reflection sheets. Blank green (or other pastel color) "Own" Reflection sheets; paper-clips. Small (3"x3") yellow post-its; small (3"x5") yellow index cards

The goal of this session is for teams to produce a final set of "Own" Reflection sheets, for reference during the Showdown. By session end, teams should have one final (green) "Own" sheet for **each** of the team's own-side reasons. It should include the Other side's most likely counters & the team's best Rebuttal to each.

Coach: **"We'll need to have one of these sheets for each of our reasons at our fingertips during the Showdown, so we know what to come back with when they try to attack our reasons. Getting them ready is our task for today."**

Objective: Organizing Own-side Reasons

A. (5-7 min) *Team activity*. All of the "**Own**" Reflection sheets that have been produced are divided & distributed, half to each team.

Coach: **"Your task is to sort these into piles, with one pile for each of our reasons (like the cards we made earlier)."**

The team may further divide the sheets and break into small groups for this task, but then reassemble to integrate their piles, so the team produces only one pile for each Own-side reason.

B. (2 min) *Team activity*. Once team is finished, Coach prompts them to review.

Coach: **"Are you sure you have just one pile for each different reason? Double-check."**

Objective: Organizing Counters to Own-side Reasons

C. (5-10 min) *Pair discussion*. The Coach provides blank GREEN SUMMARY REFLECTION SHEETS & instructs students to place one on top of each pile & paper-clip pile.

Teams assemble into PAIRS & each pair takes a share of the piles.

Coach: **"Examine each pile, one at a time, review the Counters to our reason that are written on the sheets, & bring to the top of the pile the 1-3 sheets showing the toughest, most damaging Counters to our reason. There may be only one good Counter; there could be 2 or 3. Write a FEWEST-WORDs version of each of these Counters on the green sheet, to have ready for the Showdown.**

Move any helpful yellow EVIDENCE post-its to the Final green sheet. Make a new post-it for any new evidence you now have."

Objective: Finalizing Rebuttals

D. (10 min) *Pair discussion*.

Coach: **"Now your final step. For each green sheet, look through the old sheets & find our best COMEBACK (Rebuttal) to that Counter to our reason. Write it on the green sheet below the Counter, to have ready for the Showdown."**

E. (10 min) *Pair discussion*.

Coach: **"Exchange your piles, with green sheets on top, with another pair. Review the other pair's work. Have your teammates written on the green sheet the best, strongest Comeback to each Counter, the one that will best save our reason? Is there a better Comeback or a better way to say this one? If so, make suggestions to the other pair."**

Exchanges across pairs can be continued as time permits. Suggestions by one pair to another can be made verbally or by (a new color) post-it.

F. (3-5 min) *Team discussion*. The team reviews the full set of green sheets & agrees on the final set.

G. (5 min) *Optional full-group discussion*. Coach solicits responses from entire group: **"What's their toughest counter for us to rebut? How will we do it?"**

Coach: *Separate green sheets from piles and save for team's use in Showdown.*

Showdown: 1 session

Materials needed: stopwatch; previous materials prepared by students; audio or video recording device

Pro & Con teams assemble together, seated on opposite sides of the room. The A & B teams within each toss a coin (or Coach assigns) which one will be in charge first. A coin toss determines whether Pro or Con team speaks first. The team not in charge observes and may pass notes to the team in charge but are otherwise silent. Coach reviews Showdown rules. (See Supplementary Materials.) Colored summary reflection sheets from previous sessions are distributed to each team (and other earlier materials made accessible), and the teams are offered an initial 5-10-min "huddle" to get organized and decide their strategy and a tentative order of speakers.

Debrief: 1 session

Materials needed: video viewing equipment if students are to be shown a recording of part of the showdown; copies of a transcription of selected portions of the showdown

Begin the session with 10 min of silent review of the **Argument Map** (one side's statements appearing in the left column and the other side's in the right) segment that has been distributed. Beginning students at first won't be ready to do so, but by the end of year 1 students should be able to make judgments regarding the merit of each argument move and make penciled notations of these. Coach then leads students through a discussion of why each statement was scored the way it was by the adults who did the scoring. Students can object to a particular scoring, with others invited to respond, as long as this discussion remains productive. A student who remains dissatisfied can be invited to submit a written argument for consideration by an expert judge who will make the final scoring decision.

Potential talking points and scoring:

- Did a statement **ignore** what the opponent had just said to introduce a new idea? (0 points)
- Did a statement **counter** what the opponent had said in a way that **weakened** it? (1 point)
- Did a response to a counter (rebuttal) restore strength to the speaker's point? (1 point)
- Did the speaker make an **unwarranted assumption**? (minus 1 point)
- If **evidence** was cited, was it used in the **service** of an argument (not just cited)? (1 point)

(Evidence cited but not used can be awarded ½ point.)

At the end of the session, coaches announce as a winner the side having the larger number of points based on their scoring of the showdown. Students can be advised to consult individually outside of class regarding the scoring of any particular segment that was not covered during the class debrief.

Final essay: 1 session or as a homework assignment

In a final individual essay assignment, students may take either the pro or con position, regardless of the side they took during the activity.

Appendix 3

■ ■ ■

Supplementary Materials

A. Showdown Rules

TEAM ASSIGNMENT

- Each team (A & B) will get a turn for their members to gather at the "hot table" and serve in the "hot seat." The moderator will indicate the half-way point when teams change.

"HOT-SEAT" ROLE

- A team may choose among themselves who goes to the "hot seat," except…

- No team member may take a second turn in the hot seat until every member who wishes to has had a turn.

USE OF REFLECTION SHEETS

- Students in the "hot seat" are not allowed to use written materials while debating their opponent.

- The team members at the active "hot table" are allowed to use and refer to their summary reflection sheets or other materials as desired. These may also be used/referenced during a huddle.

RULES FOR THE HOT SEAT

- Students will be allowed two (2) minutes in the "hot seat" to debate an opposing team member.

- If a huddle is called, the clock stops on these two minutes until the debate resumes.

- The student in the "hot seat" is not allowed to read from index cards or reflection sheets.

RULES FOR THE HOT SEAT (cont'd)

- A huddle may be called by anyone on either side of the debating team, including the student in the "hot seat." Wait until a speaker has finished speaking before calling a huddle.

- REMEMBER THAT YOU DO NOT LOSE POINTS FOR CALLING A HUDDLE AND TAKING TIME TO THINK ABOUT AN APPROPRIATE RESPONSE TO YOUR OPPONENT.

- When a huddle is called, the student in the "hot seat" joins their team at the table and are allowed to conference for one (1) minute.

Students review these guidelines before the Showdown:

(DOs) Your team will EARN POINTS if you...	(DON'Ts) Your team will LOSE POINTS if you...
✔ Listen well to what your opponent says ✔ Address and counter what your opponent said ✔ Take time to think about a suitable response before speaking. You do not gain points simply because you responded quickly.	✘ Ignore what your opponent says ✘ Fail to respond to your opponent while there is still time on the clock; you will not be penalized if time runs out ✘ Raise your voice at your opponent or fail to give them a reasonable chance to respond

B. Reflection sheets (Own & Other)

Team members _____

Date _____

Let's think...Starting with our argument

One of our MAIN ARGUMENTS was:

_____

_____

_____

_____

Their COUNTERARGUMENT against our argument was:

_____

_____

_____

Our COMEBACK was:

_____

_____

_____

How can this COMEBACK be improved? Is there a more effective comeback?

_____

_____

_____

_____

Team members _____

Date _____

Let's think...Starting with the other side's argument

One of the other side's
MAIN ARGUMENTS was:

_____

_____

_____

Our COUNTERARGUMENT
against their argument was:

_____

_____

_____

Give a specific example of an
improved, more effective
COUNTERARGUMENT.

_____

_____

_____

_____

C. Summary Reflection Sheets

"Other" Summary Reflection Sheet (Pink)

THEIR ARGUMENT:

OUR BEST COUNTERARGUMENT:

ANOTHER COUNTERARGUMENT:

"Own" Summary Reflection Sheet (Green)

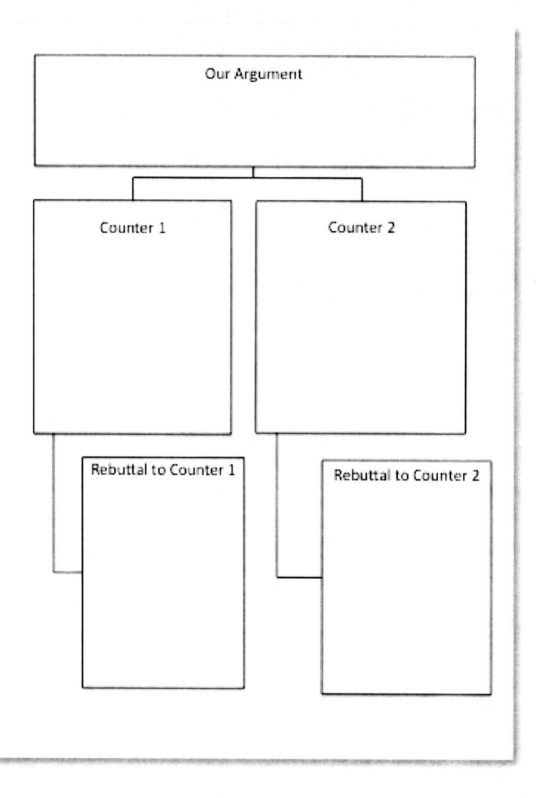

D. Optional Prediction Sheet

Names: _____   Date: _____

WHAT WILL THE OTHER SIDE SAY?

Prediction: _____

_____

Correct (circle):   Yes   No

Prediction: _____

_____

Correct (circle):   Yes   No

Prediction: _____

_____

Correct (circle):   Yes   No

Prediction: _____

_____

Correct (circle):   Yes   No

Prediction: _____

_____

Correct (circle):   Yes   No

Prediction: _____

_____

Correct (circle):   Yes   No

Prediction: _____

_____

Correct (circle):   Yes   No

Prediction: _____

_____

Correct (circle):   Yes   No

Total number correct:_____

E. Optional Pre-write Activity

Turning Your Essay Pre-write Into An Excellent Persuasive Essay

During class you "argued with yourself" about our topic, _____. You chose one position that you support and an opposing position you disagree with and then had an argument between the two sides. Below is an example of such an argument, on the topic of home schooling.

I: I think Aris should be homeschooled because it should be a parent's choice how and where their children are educated.

Me: On the other hand, parents don't always choose to do what's best for their children, and the government needs to step in at those times.

I: But if the government decides that parents aren't making good decisions, they can intervene; but for the most part parents should be allowed to choose.

Me: On the other hand, how is the government going to be able to monitor every parent who decides to homeschool their child? It's an enormous task.

I: Yes, so the government would only be able to intercede if they REALLY needed to, which is how it should be. Parents should make decisions about their children unless they're REALLY unable to. Otherwise it's a restriction of their rights.

The purpose of the pre-write activity is to think through the reasons on both sides of the issue with the intention of incorporating those reasons, counterarguments and rebuttals into a final position essay. In the case of the above argument (assuming I favor permitting home school), I have considered the argument that parents may not make the best choice and addressed that issue. Thus, the following paragraph could appear in my essay:

Homeschooling is a controversial practice that some people think should be illegal. However, if parents wish to keep their child at home they should be able to. It is the parents' right to decide for their child, and that includes deciding where the child receives an education.

Some would say that parents sometimes make decisions that aren't in the child's best interest. That may be true, and if a parent is truly negligent then the government has the right and duty to intercede. Normally, however, it is not the government's right or role to intercede in parenting decisions.

Remember, the most persuasive essays are the ones that do not pretend that its own position is the only one that has any validity and ignore the opponent's position. An essay that has the power to persuade respects and carefully considers the opposing position but refutes its major points.

Enjoy writing your essay. It's a statement of your own most complete and best thinking.

Appendix 4

. . .

Examples of Argument Maps with Scoring

(Used During Debrief Session)

Year 1 – Home School Topic

	Home School	Town School	Strategy
1	I think that Nick should learn at home because this is the US and he should have the right to do that.		Opening claim and reason
2		Yeah, but will he be able to socialize? And when he grows up he has to go out of the house right?	New ideas, but fails to address and counter the point that "he should have the right" 0
3	If he needs to find a job and learn English he can just hire a tutor.		Attempt to counter, but fails to address and counter "he has to go out of the house" 0
4		Yeah but the tutor will have to teach him English and the parents would have to pay for the tutor when there are tutors at school.	Attempt to counter, but doesn't address need to find adulthood job as reason to learn English 0 Unwarranted assumption –1
5	How do you know the tutors are provided by the school?		Counters by identifying an unwarranted assumption. +1
6		How do you know the tutors aren't provided by the school?	Attempt to counter, but unwarranted assumption has already been identified. 0
7	What if there isn't? Ok, let's say the tutor is provided at school. Even if the tutor is funded at school Nick may not want to go there. He might want to stay home with his parents and learn from the tutor.		Successful counter. Concedes point of tutor availability but undermines its relevance by reintroducing factor of Nick's wishes. +1
8		But he might be able to interact with other students speaking English or else it will be like being at jail not being able to talk to other people. '	Attempt to counter, but doesn't address central claim re Nick's wishes. 0
9	He could learn English first at home and then go socialize.		Successful counter (Nick doesn't have to attend school to socialize.) +1
10		But his parents don't know English.	Successful rebuttal (counters opponent's counter, restoring strength of #8) +1

Year 1 – Expulsion Topic

	Stay	Expel	Strategy
29	If they get expelled they will know they have a permanent record and they won't care they will be like if I get this then what is the point and they will keep on misbehaving.		New idea 0
30		But what if they go to a school that's more strict?	Successful counter +1
31	Well, then it doesn't matter because some kids they don't learn.		Attempt to counter ('some kids' is not 'all kids' so #30 is not weakened) 0
32		Well they can learn by getting expelled.	Successful counter +1
33	Well, can they learn by getting suspended?		Attempt to counter (doesn't address #32) 0
34		I don't know.	Lost opportunity to further the argument 0
35	Well, they can because getting suspended making you think about what you've done. Expelling gets you completely out of the school and that's the only school in that town. So that's a bad thing because then it is making the parents waste money and moving away to another town or city.		Successful counter +1
36		Yeah but they've been warned and their parents have been called and they are still misbehaving.	Attempt to counter (doesn't weaken #35 that suspension may be effective alternative to expulsion) 0
37	Well honestly we have all been given warnings and look some of us still misbehave. So even though if they get warnings and then they get disciplined and all of this some of them won't learn. But if they get suspended or detention they will learn that if they keep on doing this that they are going to be concealed in school.		Successful rebuttal (counters opponent's attempted counter, restoring strength of #35) +1
38		Yeah but detention is nothing; it's just like one or two hours.	Attempt to counter (doesn't address suspension alternative) 0
39	That's not always true because when I'm in detention I'm not allowed to talk, I'm only allowed to do my homework and if I do something then they call my parents saying I get suspension.		Successful rebuttal (counters opponent's attempted counter, restoring strength of #37) +1
40		Well, um yeah but well detention and suspension are different than expelling because you can come back to school. But I do not think they will learn.	Attempt to counter (doesn't justify claim that suspension alternative will be ineffective) 0

Year 2 – Organ Sale Topic

	Sell	Don't Sell	Strategy
1		People should not be able to sell their kidneys because it puts both of them in danger of diseases and that person who has one kidney if they lose their kidney that could also put them in danger.	New idea 0
2	Well evidence says that for every 3 out of 10,000 donors have problems as a result of kidney failure and the people who receive the kidney have to take medication for their entire lives and may have fatigue.		Cites evidence but doesn't use it in the service of an argument (could be agreeing it's dangerous or saying it's not because only 3) + ½
3		Well, if you just buy kidneys then the richest people are going to be able to skip everybody and then there's not going to be a line anymore. No matter how long you've been waiting if the person or friend behind you all the way in the back has a lot of money they can just get the kidney first.	Unconnected new idea –1 (Note failure to address opponent's previous statement begins to receive a negative score in year 2, reflecting a tightening of standards)
4	If we make selling kidneys legal then more people will want to sell their kidney because they'll get money so the supplies of kidneys will go up. So even if richer people buy them from the top there will be more kidneys so that poorer people can also get kidneys.		Successful counter + 1
5		But if everybody starts selling their kidneys and then you're going to have all of these left over kidneys, what are you going to do with them?	Unwarranted assumption –1
6	There's millions of people who need kidneys. I'm sure there won't be leftovers.		Successful counter + 1 But inaccurate citation of evidence 0
7		If everybody just starts giving away one of their kidneys then everybody is going to start needing kidneys.	Unwarranted assumption –1
8	Well, people can survive with only one kidney. As I said before evidence says that only 3 in 10,000 people who give up their kidney have kidney failure as a result.		Successful counter + 1 Successful use of evidence + 1

(new speakers)

	Sell	Don't Sell	Strategy
9		Selling kidneys is already illegal so that means that the transplant can't be done in a hospital so it either has to be with the doctor that doesn't have a license or with someone that isn't professional trained which puts both people at risk.	Attempt to counter (doesn't address evidence in #8 that risk is low) 0
10	Well the point of arguing for this is that we want it to be legal so since we want it to be legal and people make it legal then it will be with doctors who are trained and people don't really lose their kidneys on their black market as far as I'm concerned.		Successful counter +1
11		Even if we do make it legal there's people that are not that wealthy and are not going to be able to pay for their kidneys. The minimum that we found was like 7,000 and most kidneys are sold for like 40,000 to 50,000 dollars and that's a lot for many people.	Attempt to counter (lacks solid connection to #10) 0 Successful use of evidence +1
12	Yeah. Since there would be two systems if kidney selling became legal the people who couldn't afford to buy one would go on the [donor] list.		Successful counter +1
13		But that would still make the wait a long time and even if there are a bunch of people who are poor so either way they would suffer waiting.	Successful counter +1
14	So they would still be waiting for it if there was no kidney selling. If it was legal to sell kidneys then more people would get them and less people would die.		Successful counter +1
15		But that wouldn't be fair. If you make selling kidneys legal then the rich people would be able to get the kidney whenever they want then when they really need it while the poor people still have to wait in line just cause they can't afford it.	Successful counter +1
16	So you would rather more people die?		Successful counter +1
17		But that wouldn't be happening. Only rich people would be getting it. Right now there's more poor people than rich people.	Successful counter +1
18	Well, at least the rich people would be getting kidneys.		Successful counter +1
19		Alright, but that's just a few more of the whole population that there is that are getting kidneys.	Successful counter +1

Year 2 – China One-Child Policy Topic

	Against Policy	In Favor of Policy	Strategy
1	The one-child policy causes many problems. For example, since the one child policy began, 60 million children have gone missing.		New idea 0
2		The 60 million children that have gone missing haven't gone missing because of the one child policy. There's a prejudice against girls and who knows, maybe boys, and it's not only because of the one child policy.	Successful counter +1 Successful use of evidence +1
3	Like I said, in the evidence it said specifically that since the one child policy began, 60 million children have gone missing.		Attempt to counter (doesn't address #2) 0
4		Those kids who gone missing were like…that thing's really not definite because of the one child policy. It says in the evidence. And also, like, things like water crisis haven't begun because of the one child policy, it began because of pollution. So, it's not only because of that.	Successful counter +1 Successful use of evidence +1
5	Well, first of all, in the evidence it doesn't necessarily say that it's because of the one child policy but it says since the one child policy became, and that may be true about a million, but 60 million is hard to miss. And also, the pollution has nothing, well it may have something to do with the overpopulation but it also has things to do with like the dirt in the air.		Successful counter +1 Successful use of evidence +1
6		Well, like, it's not definite, so you just can't say it's the one child policy, and pollution has a lot to do with water, like people throwing stuff in water, like that.	Identifies unwarranted assumption +1

(new speakers)

	Against Policy	In Favor of Policy	Strategy
7	The problem with the water doesn't have anything necessarily to do with the population, but it's more of a pollution problem. So if it's a pollution problem, so why is the one child policy even being related to the water problem.		Attempt to counter (doesn't connect successfully to #6) 0
8		Well, common sense says that if there are more people then there's going to be more pollution. If there's less, like if there's only one person then he can't pollute the whole world by himself, but if there's billions of people, they can pollute the world easily.	Successssful counter (connects pollution to overpopulation problem) +1
9	But I think that there could've been a better approach to the pollution problem than saying that "oh you can only have one birth." Such as, they could've actually taught the people of China how to be… (CALLS HUDDLE)		Successssful counter +1
10	Okay, so in response to your argument, first of all look in America; it has a lot of people but we still are figuring out how to lessen the pollution.		Successssful counter +1
11		Well China has much more people than America, because China has 1.5 billion people compared to America who only has 300 million. So there's much more of an overpopulation problem in China than there is in America.	Successssful counter +1 Successful use of evidence +1
12	Yea, but don't you think that there could be other solutions to this than by just say, restricting people to have only one birth. Such as, they can try to make new industries in China since they are so ecofriendly.		Successssful counter +1
13		They aren't as ecofriendly as they could be. So, the more people there are, the more, like, pollution there's gonna be because the pollution is actually caused by the people. Therefore the one child policy is actually helping because if there's less people, there will obviously be less pollution.	Successssful counter +1

Appendix 5

■ ■ ■

Topic Suggestions

THE 25 TOPICS LISTED BELOW ALL FEATURE THE TWO MOST IMPORTANT QUALITIES for a productive topic: a rich set of arguments on both sides of the issue and a good deal of available evidence that is not too technical for students to understand and employ.

The list begins with "home schooling" and "expulsion," two topics that we have used repeatedly and successfully to introduce middle-school students to the argument curriculum. From these we typically progress to issues of broader scope, looking beyond the school world to national and even global concerns such as organ sales and foreign aid. Teachers may also wish to use topics of their own, perhaps to coordinate with a particular unit in their own curriculum. This will be particularly the case for science topics, which we therefore have not included.

In the two appendices that follow we provide Q&A lists and short readings to accompany a few of these topics.

1. **Home school.** A new town is being formed in an undeveloped area, with lots of things to decide. One important issue that has come up right away is school for children. A good school has been set up that parents and children are happy with and all children are expected to attend through high school. Houses are far apart, and school gives children a chance to be together.

   A problem has come up. The Costa family has moved to the edge of town from far away Greece with their 11-year-old son Nick. Nick was a good student and soccer player back home in Greece. Nick's parents have decided that in this new place, they want to teach Nick at home. The family speaks only Greek, and they think Nick will do better if he sticks to his family's language, and they say they can teach him everything he needs. What should happen? Is it okay for the Costa family to live in the town but keep Nick at home, or should they send their son to the town school like all the other families do?

2. **Expulsion.** Doris and Roger at the school have been misbehaving at school and disrupting the classroom. Even though they have been given warnings, their behavior does not improve. The school has told them and their parents that if they cannot follow the rules, they will be expelled. Expulsion is permanent and means that they can never come back to the school. They will have to be home-schooled or look for a school in another town. Should the school expel the misbehaving kids or should they allow these children to stay?

3. **Animal research.** Should scientists be allowed to experiment on animals in research laboratories?

4. **Organ sale.** New kidneys are in short supply; people needing them often have to wait years for a donation. A couple knows of someone who is near death and desperate for a new kidney and will pay them $25,000 to sell him one. The husband wants to do it because they are very poor and need the money to feed their family, but the wife is worried it could cause problems. Should people be allowed to sell their kidneys?

5. **China one-child policy.** China is so overpopulated that the country can no longer take care of everyone. To try to solve this problem and improve everyone's access to goods and services, China began a one-child policy. This means that each couple is allowed to have only one child. Should China have this one-child policy?

6. **Juvenile justice.** Teens who commit serious crimes may be tried and sentenced in the adult court system. Or they may be tried in a court system for juveniles. Which is better?

7. **Abortion.** Should abortion be allowed?

8. **Euthanasia.** Should euthanasia be allowed if it is a person's wish to end their life?

9. **Capital punishment.** Should the death penalty be allowed for serious crimes?

10. **Aid to foreign nations.** A poor Asian country is being invaded by a neighboring country that wants to take it over. It has asked the United States to send soldiers to help. The US is not sure it has enough soldiers available to send and is concerned about the cost in dollars and lives. Throughout its history, the US has had to decide whether to involve itself in another country's problems. Some think the US should act in these situations. Others think we should use our resources on our own serious problems at home. Should the US get involved or focus on problems at home?

11. **Energy conservation.** Should large cars be outlawed to conserve energy?

12. **Athlete infractions.** Should athletes who use illegal substances be banned from their sport for life?

13. **GM foods.** Should genetically modified foods be produced and sold?

14. **Royalties.** Should downloading of music and videos without payment to authors be illegal?

15. **Video games.** Should some video games be outlawed for sale to children or teens?

16. **Drug use.** Illegal drug use can be fought with tougher punishments on drug users or on drug suppliers. Which will be most effective in reducing illegal drug use?

17. **End-of-life care.** Should the government put limits on how much government health care programs like Medicare should spend on very expensive drugs that give dying people only a few extra months of life?

18. **Food choice.** Should a tax be imposed on soft drinks and that money go to reducing the prices of healthy foods?

19. **Prison conditions.** Should prisons be designed to make prisoners' lives more comfortable, with things like TVs, music systems, and sports?

20. **Torture.** Is torture of prisoners ever justified?

21. **Aid to abusers.** There is evidence the Afghan National Army (ANA) torture their prisoners. Should Americans be helping to train and support the ANA?

22. **Health insurance.** Should the U.S. government require people to have health insurance?

23. **Medical care.** Should people without insurance be treated in emergency rooms and hospitals for free?

24. **Malpractice.** Should people win large amounts of money for malpractice in medical lawsuits involving loss of life or major bodily damage?

25. **Elder care.** Should the government take care of old people who don't have enough money to live or should the old person's grown children be required to take care of them?

Appendix 6

■ ■ ■

Sample Evidence Q&A Sets

Animal Testing Topic

Initial set provided to students

Q. Why are animals useful in medical research?

A. Animal organs often resemble human organs, so treatments can be expected to work in similar ways.

Q. Why are new products sometimes tested on animals?

A. To make sure they are safe before they are made available to humans.

Q. How humanely are animals treated in laboratories?

A. There are laws in place to help ensure that distress and pain in animals is kept to a minimum, but the daily treatment of animals is not known for certain because the testing places cannot be monitored at all times.

Q. Has animal testing led to cures for any human diseases?

A. Animal testing has led to treatments and cures for many human diseases. For example, research with dogs led to treatments for diabetes, research with armadillos led to leprosy vaccines, and research with monkeys has led to treatments for hepatitis, polio, and AIDS.

Q. Are there other ways to find treatments for diseases without using animals?

A. Some scientists develop computer models. Others ask for human volunteers to participate in trials of new treatments.

Q. Can medical testing of animals be of any benefit to animals?

A. Many of the medications that are given to sick animals (such as pets and zoo animals) were discovered as a result of medical research on animals.

Q. Does research on animals do the animals any harm?

A. In some cases the procedures have been reported to be harmless to the animals; in other cases effects have been reported to be very serious, even leading to death. Often animals are put to death when an experiment is finished.

Q. How many animals are involved in medical research each year in the USA?

A. Regulations require that scientists use as few animals as possible. According to the U.S. Department of Agriculture (USDA), 1.2 million animals were used in 2005. This does not include rats and mice, which make up about 90% of research animals.

Q. Are treatments discovered through animal testing always effective when they are used with humans?

A. Sometimes treatments that work for the animals tested are not effective for humans. This may be because differences between the animal and humans are not well understood, or because different amounts of a medicine cause different effects when they are used with humans.

Q. What kinds of animals are involved in medical research?

A. Rats and mice account for about 95 percent of all animals used in research. Others include rabbits, guinea pigs, hamsters, farm animals, fish and insects. Cats are most often used in brain research, while dogs are most often used in heart and bone research. Choice of animal for a specific study depends on how close the animal's organs and bodily functions are to those of humans.

Note. Students have not yet begun to generate their own questions for this early topic.

Kidney Sale Topic
Initial set provided to students

Q. What is a kidney and what does it do?

A. Kidneys are two bean-shaped organs about the size of a fist. They are located near the middle of your back, just below the rib cage. Every day, your kidneys process about 200 quarts of blood to sift out about 2 quarts of waste products and extra water. The waste and extra water become urine,

Q. How many people need a new kidney in the USA?

A. In 2005, approximately 78,000 people in the USA were on the waiting list for a new kidney.

Q. Do people need both their kidneys?

A. No, an otherwise healthy person can live with just one kidney. However, if that kidney fails, the person cannot survive without at least one kidney..

Q. Do people die because they can't get a kidney in time?

A. Yes, in 2005, 3000 people in the USA died while waiting for a kidney.

Q. Is it illegal to buy and sell kidneys?

A. Organ sales are illegal in many countries but legal in others. They are currently illegal in the USA.

Q. How do people in the USA currently get a kidney?

A. Names of people who need a kidney are placed on a list and they wait for a kidney from someone who has agreed to donate theirs. Most donations come from people who agreed to be organ donors and have recently died. Or Americans can travel to a country where kidney sales are allowed, buy a kidney there, and have surgery there to put it in.

Q. How is it decided who is next in line for a donated kidney?

A. Generally the people who have been waiting the longest are the next in line.

Q. Is age a factor in deciding who is most deserving of a donated kidney?

A. Generally only length on the waiting list, not age, determines who gets a kidney. This means that a young donor's kidney may go to an old person, rather than to a younger person who would use it for more years.

Q. What are the health risks to those who give a kidney?

A. Those who give a kidney may experience only fatigue (tiredness). But 3 in every 10,000 of these people will die from kidney failure.

Q. What are the health risks to those who receive another person's kidney?

A. Those who have received a new kidney must take medication for the rest of their lives to avoid complications.

Sample of one class's student-generated questions (with the answers provided to students)

Q. Before you donate a kidney, do you get checked to make sure you are healthy and your kidney works well?

A. Yes, a thorough medical evaluation is done before the surgery to insure not only the kidney is healthy, but also that the patient is healthy enough to endure the surgery and live with only one kidney.

Q. Is it illegal to sell kidneys?

A. Yes, it is illegal to sell kidneys in the United States.

Q. How many people who gave their kidneys away have problems now?

A. It is very difficult to track down everyone who has donated a kidney. However, the University of Minnesota did a study on the survival of the 3,698 people who had donated a kidney there since 1963. They randomly selected 255 donors and performed a series of tests on them to determine if their kidneys were functioning properly; 11 experienced kidney failure and the rest were generally healthy.

Q. Will giving a kidney away affect you?

A. Risks of kidney donation include the risk of anesthesia, bleeding, infection, and wound healing problems. The usual recovery time after the surgery is short, and donors can generally resume their normal lives within 2 to 6 weeks. Kidney donation, most often, does not change your lifestyle. It does not change the length of your life or increase risk of getting kidney disease. It does not interfere with a woman's ability to have children. You will not need to change your diet or take additional medicines. The other kidney will grow and take over the work of both kidneys. Some long-term studies of kidney donors have shown that protein in the urine or high blood pressure may occur after giving a kidney. Other large studies of kidney donors have shown that there is no increased risk of kidney failure after donating a kidney. However, were you to have kidney failure, you wouldn't have another healthy kidney to rely on.

Q. If you have insurance, does it pay for a kidney transplant and the kidney if you need it?

A. Yes, insurance most always covers the cost of this operation.

Q. Has anyone been forced to give a kidney to another person?

A. Despite rumors, there is no firm evidence that force has occurred, which would be a violation of human rights; but someone might feel pressured to give one.

Q. How long do you have to replace a damaged kidney before you die?

A. Kidneys can be damaged due to a number of different reasons and to varying degrees. Such differences affect the body differently, so the length of time that one can live with a damaged kidney is different in every case.

Q. Is there any research showing that more people will give their kidney if they get paid?

A. No such research is available.

Q. If someone in your family is sick and needs a kidney, is it still considered illegal if you give it free of charge?

A. No it is not illegal, and such donations occur.

Q. Is it legal to currently donate kidneys in the U.S.?

A. Yes, it is legal to donate kidneys. It is not legal to receive money in exchange for your kidneys. In the US, each state regulates the process of organ donation, and the system is purely on a "consent" basis, where you must actively state that you wish to donate your kidney. Many states also encourage donations by allowing the consent to be noted on a person's driver's license.

Q. Do people who sell their kidneys benefit from the money they receive?

A. Since the donor receiving the money has the freedom to spend or save the money however they choose, and there is no record of how this money gets spent, there is no way to measure whether the donor actually benefits from the money they receive, but the money they do receive is often substantial and has the potential to benefit them in various ways.

Q. Is it legal to sell kidneys in other countries?

A. At this time the only country to legalize selling kidneys is Iran. Some other countries are considering legalizing such sales. evidence is available that this has happened.

Q. What kinds of diseases can affect a kidney? Is there a cure for these diseases?

A. There are over a hundred different diseases that can affect a kidney. Some have cures, and others don't. The most common problems are kidney stones, kidney infections and kidney failure as a result of diabetes. Kidney stones and kidney infections can be treated; kidney failure is chronic and has no cure.

Q. Does allowing organ sales make it easy to get one if needed?

A. The case of Iran suggests it does. Kidney sales are allowed in Iran and there is currently no wait to get one there.

Q. Do some people make money by buying and selling organs?

A. Yes, there is evidence in some countries that "middle-men" buy a kidney from a very poor person and then sell it to someone needing a kidney for a much higher price.

Q. How many Americans would have to agree to donate a kidney in order to eliminate a waiting list?

A. If less than one-tenth of one percent of American adults donated a kidney, there would be no shortage.

Q. Are there ways to increase organ donations?

A. Studies have shown that in an "opt out" system in which they check a box on their driver's license only if they do NOT want to donate organs when they die, most people agree to be donors. However, people are much less likely to check a box that asks them to "opt in" to an organ donation registry.

Q. If organ sales are allowed, can a country's government regulate the practice so no one is taken advantage of?

A. Iran reports success in regulating kidney sales. The Charity Association for the Support of Kidney Patients (CASKP) and the Charity Foundation for Special Diseases (CFSD) control kidney sales. The organizations match donors to recipients, setting up tests to ensure compatibility and regulating prices.

Q. Does making organ sales against the law lead to dishonest practices to get around the law?

A. There is evidence this happens. For example, if a country's law says people can only donate a kidney to a family member, people have gotten married, or one has adopted the other, so they become family members who can donate to one another.

China One-Child Policy Topic

Initial set provided to students

Q. Have any countries tried other methods to control their population?

A. Yes. Some methods have had some success, but all methods have problems. For example, educating people about the problems of overpopulation has not had much success.

Q. What has happened to the size of China's population since it instituted its one child policy in 1979?

A. China estimates that it has three to four hundred million fewer people today than it would have if it never began the one child policy. Even though there are fewer people in China than there would be without the policy, China's population is still growing and is expected to reach 1.5 billion people.

Q. How much did China's population grow in the years before the one child policy?

A. From 1949 to 1979, China's population increased from about 540 million to more than 800 million.

Q. How have living conditions changed since the one child policy began?

A. Since the one child policy began, many problems that come with overpopulation have become less severe. There have been fewer epidemics, and improvements in health services, education, housing, law enforcement, and the environment.

Q. What happens if a Chinese family has twins?

A. The one child policy is actually a "one birth" policy; parents are permitted to give birth one time even it results in multiple children. Parents who have twins are given the same benefits as parents of one child.

Q. How many children did most Chinese families have before the one child policy?

A. In the early 1970s, the average woman in China had five children. Today, the average woman has 1.6 children.

Q. What if a Chinese family does not agree with the one child policy?

A. A Chinese family would have to accept the penalties that come with having a second child. These include large fines, ranging from half to ten times a person's annual salary.

Q. Do people in China agree with the one child policy and accept it?

A. One study found that 75% of the Chinese population supports the one child policy, but we cannot know for sure because people in China do not, in general, criticize government policies.

Sample of one class's student-generated questions (with the answers provided to students)

Q. Does disease rise with overpopulation?

A. Yes, high population densities cause epidemics.

Q. If a child dies, can the couple have another?

A. Since the policy is to control the population, if a child dies, another one can replace this child; so yes, the couple can have another child in this case.

Q. If the couple wants to have more than one child, can they move out of the country?

A. Yes, a family can decide to immigrate to another country and move to a country where this policy does not exist.

Q. What if someone gets pregnant by accident?

A. If the mother decides she does not want to raise the child, she must either have an abortion or give the child to an orphanage.

Q. Is there prejudice against girl babies?

A. Yes, there have been cases in which abortions have taken place because the parents want a boy. In many cases, families who live in rural locations feel the need to have boys to take care of family responsibilities. However, in Shanghai, this discrimination is not a widespread issue. A survey was given to 3,500 parents in Shanghai who were expecting a child. Most parents did not have a preference of the gender but for those who did, 15% wanted girls and 12% wanted boys.

Q. What is the population of the U.S. versus China and how much bigger is the land?

A. China has a population of over 1.3 billion. The US has just over 300 million. In terms of size, the United States is about 9,631,418 km² and China is about 9,596,960 km².

Q. What type of government is China (communist, capitalist)?

A. China is a communist state.

Q. What is the average home size in China?

A. In 2008, China had about 28 square meters (or about 91 square feet) of floor space per person in cities and towns. Housing in rural areas reached about 32 square meters (or 104 square feet) of space per person.

Q. How has per capita GDP in China grown or fallen since the one-child policy?

A. China's GDP per capita grew from less than $400 (US) in 1978 to an estimated $8,288 (US) in 2011.

Q. How does China enforce the one-child policy?

A. If couples have a second child, they must pay fines that can range from one half to ten times their annual salary. There have also been reports of forced sterilizations and abortions. In 2002, China outlawed the use of physical force to make a woman submit to an abortion or sterilization, but some local governments still demand abortions if the pregnancy violates local regulations. Enforcement of one-child policies varies greatly from place to place in China.

Q. Can China currently support all its people with healthcare and retirement?

A. The public pension (retirement) system covers only a fraction of the population. The Chinese culture relies heavily on their children for support in the future. It is said that without reform of the public pension system, tens of millions of Chinese could arrive at old age over the next few decades without pensions and with inadequate family support.

Q. What are the problems associated with overpopulation?

A. Most biologists and sociologists see overpopulation as a serious threat to the quality of human life. Overpopulation can lead to problems such as:

- New diseases and epidemics
- Environmental problems like pollution and soil contamination
- Inadequate fresh water
- Loss of farmable land
- High infant and child mortality
- Starvation and malnutrition
- Low life expectancy
- Elevated crime rate
- Unhygienic living conditions if there is little fresh water or if there are no sewers.

Q. What happens if a couple does not register their child or their second child to the government?

A. If the government finds, out, they will have to pay a fine based on the income of the family and other factors. Children not registered with the government cannot obtain birth certificates or proper documentation. Without proper papers these children cannot enter school or find work as adults.

Q. Is China running out of resources due to overpopulation?

A. China does have a water shortage crisis which is due, in part, to overpopulation and other often related factors like pollution. This is especially true in the northern region of China, where 11 provinces are said to be in "water poverty" according to the World Bank. Currently, approximately 300 million people living in rural China are without safe drinking water. The water shortage also affects China's food supply, since many crops must be irrigated with polluted water; this can mean low crop yields and unhealthy food. Lack of water also affects the food supply by limiting the amount of grass available for livestock (like cattle).

Q. How many multiple births (twins, triplets) are born in China every year?

A. According to ABC World News, official statistics on China's multiple births are currently not available, but the Yangzhou Evening News used Dr. Zhang's hospital as an example of the rate of multiple births. The hospital had 24 twin births among 1600 mothers last year, which the newspaper called, "a proportion of twins born beyond the laws of nature." They suspect this increase to be due to mothers taking fertility medications to have twins since families are not punished for multiple births, if it is their first birth.

Q. If a couple has one child and then divorces, can either the father or mother have another child with a new spouse?

A. The rules differ by province, but in some provinces, if a couple divorces, either person may have a second child if they marry someone who has never had a child of his/her own.

Q. Once a child is "of age" (considered an adult) can their parents have a second child?

A. No.

Q. What is China's population right now?

A. As of November 1st 2010, China's population is 1,339,724,852.

Q. How many Chinese people come to the United States to give birth to a second child?

A. Thousands of Chinese apply for political asylum to the US each year by asserting that being limited to one child is a form of political persecution. In 1996, US legislation declared one-child asylum claims to be valid, but it was further mandated that no more than 1000 one-child asylum pleas be granted each year.

Q. Has China tried to start being conservative with its water resources?

A. China has implemented eco-conservation programs to try to improve conditions at sources of the Yangtze River, Yellow River and Lancang River. These efforts have somewhat improved grazing conditions for farm animals. In 2011 seven Chinese cities and provinces, including the national capital Beijing, are taking local officials' water conservation efforts into account when assessing their work performances. The Chinese Ministry of Water Resources has said that officials will be "held accountable" if they fail to meet expectations, but has not stated what kinds of consequences will occur. The government also asserts that China aims to double its average annual spending on water conservation during the next decade.

Juvenile Justice Topic

Initial set provided to students

Q. What is the adult justice system?

A. The adult justice system includes the courts and prisons that try, convict, sentence, and carry out the sentence of adult offenders.

Q. What is the juvenile justice system?

A. The juvenile justice system includes the courts and juvenile detention centers that address the punishment of juvenile offenders.

Sample of one class's student-generated questions
(with the answers provided to students)

Q. What are other people's opinions about this topic?

A. A national poll in 2006 found that 55% of Americans think that juveniles should be tried in adult court; 34% think that they should not. (The rest are undecided.)

Q. What are the punishments for serious crimes in both justice systems?

A. Depending on the state, punishments in the adult justice system could include probation, therapy, community service, jail time, or even death. Within the juvenile system, punishments could include probation, therapy, community service, or jail time.

Q. How does the adult court system work?

A. In the adult court system, a defendant is given a trial with a jury. The defendant is then found "guilty" or "not guilty." If guilty, the defendant is sentenced; in the adult court system, the focus is on the punishment/ sentence, not on rehabilitation.

Q. Is there a difference between the adult court system and the adult justice system?

A. The adult court system is part of the adult justice system, which also includes law enforcement and jails.

Q. How many people get STDs in adult prison?

A. STD's in prison are slightly more common than in the general population; one study found that the number was estimated at 2.2 cases for every 100,000 inmates.

Q. Why is the adult age 18 years old?

A. The age of adulthood varies from country to country and (in some cases) state to state. The law generally recognizes that 18 years is the age of adulthood, but in some countries that is as low as 15 or as high as 21.

Q. Do people get smarter as they get older?

A. Older people in general tend to have more knowledge and wisdom, but individuals vary. Some people do not become smarter as they get older.

Q. Do children end up like their parents? If not, who/what decides how they turn out?

A. Both biology and experience affect how children turn out.

Q. Do parents choose where there children get to go to the juvenile center?

A. No. Children are assigned to a juvenile center by the judge.

Q. Which has more violence, adult jail or juvenile?

A. Both adult jail and juvenile detention centers have violence. Statistics are not reliable enough to tell us for sure which is more violent.

Q. When is the prefrontal cortex (part of brain) fully developed?

A. The prefrontal cortex, which is responsible for abstract thinking and the ability to exercise good judgment, is not fully developed until about the age of 25.

Q. Do people get physically abused in prison? If so, what is the average age group?

A. Some prisoners get physically abused by other prisoners. Age is not a factor in which prisoners are abused.

Q. Putting a child in prison could have a severe effect on their education. Will they be given tutoring or an educational program in prison?

A. Whether in juvenile detention center or in adult prison, juveniles have a legal right to educational services.

Q. How many kids went to juvenile in 2011?

A. Approximately 320,000 youths are sentenced to juvenile detention centers each year in the USA.

Q. How many adults went to adult jail in 2011?

A. Around 1 million adults are sentenced to jail each year in the USA.

Q. How many teenagers get sent to trial each year?

A. Approximately 1.6 million teens per year are sent to juvenile court in the USA.

Q. What are the conditions of Juveniles (including casualties such as riots, arguments, fist fights, etc,.)?

A. Juvenile detention centers contain many positive aspects (such as education, counseling, and rehabilitation) and many negative aspects (such as violence).

Q. What are the conditions of "adult jail (including casualties such as riots, arguments, fist fights, etc.)?"

A. Adult jail includes positive aspects (such as job training programs and rehabilitation) and negative aspects (such as violence).

Q. Is the time spent in juvenile detention shorter than it is in regular prison?

A. Though the time of a sentence varies from case to case, a teen convicted and sent to juvenile detention is released at age 18; in adult prison, there is no mandatory release date.

Q. Can you bail out of juvenile (pay to get out)?

A. Sometimes, but the right to bail is not guaranteed, and sometimes law enforcement is allowed to detain youth without bail.

Q. Why are you considered mature at age 18? (Is the brain fully developed or something?)

A. There is no biological reason to consider a person mature at age 18 (the brain is not fully developed until the 20's), but social convention says that 18 is the age of maturity for several reasons, including the fact that 18 is often the age when teens move out of their parents' house.

Q. Can a child serving prison time have a negative effect on their later life?

A. There are few statistics tracking the effect that serving time in adult prison can have on youth; however, some say that teens in adult prison will not have access to good adult role models, making it more likely that they will commit crimes later in life.

Q. In an adult jail about how much people you have in one single jail cell?

A. It depends on the jail; some have only one or two, and some house four or (occasionally) more.

Q. What is the nutrition value in adult vs juvie jail food?

A. The same companies usually provide food to both adult prison and juvenile detention centers, so the nutritional content is similar.

Q. What are some court cases about this topic? What were the outcomes?

A. One famous case was that of Joshua Phillips, who murdered an 8-year-old girl when he was 14. He was sentenced to life without parole and lost a 2002 appeal asking to be tried in juvenile court. A more recent example is that of Cristian Fernandez, a 12-year-old who was arrested in fall 2011 after beating his 2-year-old brother to death. The state of Florida asked for life without parole.

Q. What exactly is considered a serious crime and what are its punishments in the adult and juvenile court system?

A. While definitions of a serious crime vary, when youth are tried as adults, it is almost always because they killed someone. In adult court, the punishment can vary from jail time to life in prison to the death penalty. In the juvenile court system, the child would be placed in a detention center until they were 18, at which point they would be released and their records sealed.

Q. If a juvenile was put in the same prison as adults, would they share a cell? Or would they share time eating or outside together?

A. Sometimes juveniles in adult prisons are kept completely separate from the adults, but sometimes they either share cells and/or have social time with the adults.

Q. Does being in jail or juvie change your behavior?

A. While there is evidence that jail and juvenile detention centers can change behavior, there is disagreement on how they change behavior. Some argue that jail has a negative impact on behavior, making crimes worse, and some argue that it has a positive impact. The same is true for juvenile detention centers; some say that they rehabilitate troubled youth, and some say that they lead to a lifetime of crime.

Q. What is the official age range of a "juvenile"?

A. It varies from state to state; in some states, children as young as 11 or 12 have been tried as adults.

Q. What is the longest time period someone has stayed in juvenile?

A. Because records are sealed after a juvenile reaches age 18, we do not have access to that information.

Q. What is the percent of people that get mental problems when they come out of jail?

A. There have not been studies that can tell us how many people have mental problems when they are released from jail. Furthermore, there is no way to know how many people end up in jail because they have mental illness and how many develop mental illness while in jail.

Q. Can jail time affect your health in any negative or positive way?

A. There is a higher percent of illness among US prisoners than in the general US population, including STD's.

Q. What happens if a person murders or severely hurts someone in prison or juvenile jail?

A. Often, time is added on to their sentence and/or parole is denied.

Q. What happens if someone dies from a disease in jail?

A. Their body is released to their family for burial.

Q. Does the child/teen's maturity affect the outcome of the teen's verdict?

A. It may. That depends on the judge (in juvenile court) and the jury (in adult court).

Q. Does the child's age affect how much time he/she spends in jail?

A. It might. Sentencing is done on a case-by-case basis, and a child's age might be taken into account during sentencing.

Q. Based on the severity of the crime, can leisure activity or "free time" be restricted or refined in prison?

A. Though it is not the norm to restrict free time based on the severity of the crime, prisoners can have free time taken away and/or reduced based on their behavior in prison.

Q. If being bailed out of prison is an option, does the fine increase or decrease based on age? Or does it stay the same, adult or juvenile.

A. Bail is based on a variety of factors, including severity of the crime and the risk that the prisoner will leave the jurisdiction. Age is not a direct factor in deciding bail.

Q. How many kids who get out of Juvenile Prison commit crimes again?

A. Because juvenile records are sealed when the child reaches age 18, this information is not available.

Q. How many people who get out of Adult Prison commit crimes again?

A. The statistics vary, but some studies show that as many as 70% of prisoners are rearrested for another crime within 3 years of release. However, only approximately 27% of prisoners are reconvicted for another crime after release.

Q. In TV shows there are characters that easily break out of prison. Is it really that easy to break out?

A. No. In 2008, the most recent year statistics are available, 2,512 out of approximately 1.4 million prisoners escaped from prison.

Q. If you are tried as a juvenile too many times are you tried as an adult?

A. While there is not a set number of crimes a juvenile can commit before being tried as an adult, many serious crimes might cause the juvenile to be tried as an adult.

Q. Is there a limit to how old or how young you have to be to be put in juvenile or adult prison? (i.e. a 93 year-old man or a 4 year-old child)

A. There is not one single legal age limit; however, a major factor is the intent of the person who committed a crime. It is unlikely that a young child (such as a 4-year-old) would be believed to have the intent to commit a crime. These decisions are made on a case-by-case basis.

Q. Is contact with family more or less based on the form of prison?

A. It used to be that inmates in juvenile detention centers had more access to family visits than those in adult prison. However, several court cases in the 1990s changed that, and now juveniles are guaranteed the right to the same amount of family visits, phone calls, and mail whether they are in juvenile or adult prison.

Q. Do kids learn more from other kids or adults?

A. In early childhood, parents are the child's biggest influence; however, by their teen years, most adolescents are influenced by peers more than parents.

Q. What does convicted mean?

A. Someone who is convicted of a crime has gone to court and be found guilty by a jury or has pled guilty to the crime. Someone can be arrested but not convicted, if they are found not guilty by a jury, if the case is dismissed because of some other reason, or if the police decide to pursue other leads.

Q. If put in adult justice system, will their jail time increase?

A. Possibly, but not necessarily. While a juvenile tried in the adult justice system might get a short sentence, they could also get a long sentence. And a teen tried in juvenile court is guaranteed release at age 18, but in adult court they are not.

Q. What percentage of teens listen to their parents?

A. Studies show that for serious issues, teens take their parents' advice more often than not.

Q. Do some brains develop slower and ineffectively than others?

A. Yes, people's brains develop at different rates. However, most people develop in the same general pattern and in approximately the same time frame.

Q. Do you have an advantage if you are mentally disabled? What fits into the category of mentally disabled?

A. In adult court, mental disability (including an extremely low IQ, and some types of mental illness) is taken into consideration by the court and can result in a lighter sentence or a special sentence (such as being put into a mental institution instead of jail). The Supreme Court ruled that the death penalty is unconstitutional (and therefore illegal) for people with mental retardation. In juvenile court, mental disability is also taken into consideration. Juvenile courts work with the educational system to make sure that adolescents in juvenile detention centers receive special education courses and are put in an appropriate environment.

Q. Can mental problems serve as an excuse for a teen's behavior? If so does that change the outcome of where they end up?

A. The defense team for a teen could use mental illness as a defense, and that may or may not affect the outcome. For example, a girl in Missouri was sentenced to life in prison even though her defense team tried to get her a shorter sentence because she suffered from depression and was taking a drug (Prozac) that they claimed made her more violent.

Q. Is the topic we are discussing dealing with the U.S justice court or from other countries?

A. We are discussing the US justice system.

Q. What is the current law, where do children go if they commit serious crimes?

A. The law varies by state, but most states have provisions that allow for minors to be tried as adults for serious crimes.

Q. Can a child defend themselves in court?

A. Though the law varies by state, in most cases a child is required to have a lawyer for their defense.

Q. Would the government save money if they didn't have to pay for a juvenile system?

A. In theory, yes, because the cost to hold someone in adult prison for one year was estimated at $50,000, while the cost to hold someone in juvenile detention for one year is $75,000.

Appendix 7

■ ■ ■

Sample of Readings for Four Topics

Animal Testing Topic

Making Informed Choices About the Use of Animals in Testing

By Ian Murnaghan Oct. 31, 2010

http://www.aboutanimaltesting.co.uk/making-informed-choices-about-the-use-animals-in-testing.html

Animal testing affects everyone in one form or another. Each time you receive a prescription for a drug, you are likely taking a medication that was tested on animals. Each time you use a cleaning product or household item, you are also probably using a formulation that was tested on animals. Yet, many of us give little thought to the process that occurs to bring us an enormous number of consumer products and potentially life-saving medications. On the flip side, activists who aggressively target animal testing companies rarely shun all medicine and its drugs. For most of the public, it can be difficult to make an informed choice as well, given that there is a great deal of misinformation, exaggeration and manipulative explanations that slant animal testing in a light that simply is not accurate.

Animal Welfare Groups

Animal welfare groups do, in one sense, play a valuable role at times. They keep the government 'on their toes,' by monitoring the activities of regulation and challenging aspects that they feel are not conducive to humane animal care. It is the extremists and particularly aggressive activists who use intimidation, threats and physical violence, which give a dirty reputation to animal welfare groups.

At the same time, there is no shortage of manipulation within animal welfare groups with regards to exaggeration of the facts. A quick check of some of the more well-known groups such as People for the Ethical Treatment of Animals (PETA) will show the use of violent, gory words to describe standard medical acts that are performed under anaesthetic. This type of approach is used by many animal welfare groups to promote their organisation. For example, a very typical medical procedure is to take a biopsy, which could perhaps involve a tissue sample from the animal's leg. An animal welfare group may use a phrase such as 'sliced flesh from the animal's leg' to provide the reader with a very horrific and gory spin on the act. The insinuation is that the scientist ripped off part of the animal's leg while the animal was still functional. The words also imply that the animal was not provided with any pain reliever or anaesthetic.

It is suggested that you be wary of this sort of terminology when formulating an accurate understanding of animal testing. For the above example, you may fully object to the use of animal testing for biomedical research even knowing that the animal is under anaesthetic and that the procedure involves a standard biopsy. The point, however, is that you will have made an informed decision based on facts rather than one based on slanted exaggeration.

Researchers and Animal Testing

Most researchers and scientists like animals and indeed, have pets of their own that they dote on daily. The idea that they hate animals is a false one and has painted an unfair picture of those who are involved in animal testing. At the same time, there are still those researchers or animal technicians who abuse animals and do not treat them humanely and ethically. The scientific community, not just the public, condemns the researchers who commit animal abuse. Most people would agree that those who mistreat animals under testing conditions should be punished and receive consequences that are appropriate to their actions. But ultimately, these researchers are a minority - not a majority - and the coverage by the media and animal welfare groups can paint a picture of all researchers being abusive rather than a very limited minority.

Cosmetics Testing

The area of cosmetics testing is one that tends to have more opponents then supporters. This is primarily due to the aesthetic nature of cosmetics, which many people cite as frivolous and unethical in terms of its application to animal testing. Those who do support animal testing tend to support its medical applications because these benefit human life by reducing morbidity and mortality from many diseases and health conditions. You may still feel that animal testing for cosmetics is appropriate but keep in mind that it is now banned in the United Kingdom and will soon be almost fully banned in the European Union by 2009.

Your Opinion Can Make a Difference

It can be tough to weigh all sides of animal testing and even more difficult to decide if you support certain aspects and condemn others. Perhaps you will condemn all animal testing or alternately, support the use of animals for any testing purposes. Try to read and learn from as many reputable sources as possible and consider making a decision after you feel well-informed. Then, you can also consider getting involved with an organisation that aims to support or conversely, stop some or all aspects of animal testing. Even if you are uncertain about which side of animal testing you are on, you can still become informed because animal testing laws and regulations are all influenced by the public. Your reaction to animal testing is important and does impact the practice.

Kidney Sale Topic

The New York Times*
By Dan Bilefsky
Published: June 28, 2012

BELGRADE, Serbia — Pavle Mircov and his partner, Daniella, nervously scan their e-mail in-box every 15 minutes, desperate for economic salvation: a buyer willing to pay nearly $40,000 for one of their kidneys.

Ervin Balo, a father of two with his wife, Elivira, tried to sell a kidney to support his family in Kikinda, Serbia, while unemployed.

The couple, the parents of two teenagers, put their organs up for sale on a local online classified site six months ago after Mr. Mircov, 50, lost his job at a meat factory here. He has not been able to find any work, he said, so he has grown desperate. When his father recently died, Mr. Mircov could not afford a tombstone. The telephone service has been cut off. One meal a day of bread and salami is the family's only extravagance.

"When you need to put food on the table, selling a kidney doesn't seem like much of a sacrifice," Mr. Mircov said.

Facing grinding poverty, some Europeans are seeking to sell their kidneys, lungs, bone marrow or corneas, experts say. This phenomenon is relatively new in Serbia, a nation that has been battered by war and is grappling with the financial crisis that has swept the Continent. The spread of illegal organ sales into Europe, where they are gaining momentum, has been abetted by the Internet, a global shortage of organs for transplants and, in some cases, unscrupulous traffickers ready to exploit the economic misery.

In Spain, Italy, Greece and Russia, advertisements by people peddling organs — as well as hair, sperm and breast milk — have turned up on the Internet, with asking prices for lungs as high as $250,000. In late May, the Israeli police detained 10 members of an international crime ring suspected of organ trafficking in Europe, European Union law enforcement officials said. The officials said the suspects had targeted impoverished people in Moldova, Kazakhstan, Russia, Ukraine and Belarus.

"Organ trafficking is a growth industry," said Jonathan Ratel, a European Union special prosecutor who is leading a case against seven people accused of luring poor victims from Turkey and former communist countries to Kosovo to sell their kidneys with false promises of payments of up to $20,000. "Organized criminal groups are preying upon the vulnerable on both sides of the supply chain: people suffering from chronic poverty, and desperate and wealthy patients who will do anything to survive."

The main supply countries have traditionally been China, India, Brazil and the Philippines. But experts say Europeans are increasingly vulnerable.

An estimated 15,000 to 20,000 kidneys are illegally sold globally each year, according to Organs Watch, a human rights group in Berkeley, Calif., that tracks the illegal organ trade. The World Health Organization estimates that only 10 percent of global needs for organ transplantation are being met.

Nancy Scheper-Hughes, the director of Organs Watch and a professor of medical anthropology at the University of California, Berkeley, said the attempt by poor Europeans to sell their organs was reminiscent of the period after the collapse of the Soviet Union, when chronic joblessness created a new breed of willing sellers.

* Secured from the Internet

Trade in organs in Serbia is illegal and punishable by up to 10 years in prison. But that is not deterring the people of Doljevac, a poor municipality of 19,000 people in southern Serbia, where the government refused an attempt by residents to register a local agency to sell their organs and blood abroad for profit.

Violeta Cavac, a homemaker advocating for the network, said that the unemployment rate in Doljevac was 50 percent and that more than 3,000 people had wanted to participate. Deprived of a legal channel to sell their organs, she said, residents are now trying to sell body parts in neighboring Bulgaria or in Kosovo.

"I will sell my kidney, my liver, or do anything necessary to survive," she said.

Hunched over his computer in Kovin, about 25 miles from Belgrade, Mr. Mircov showed a reporter his kidney-for-sale advertisement, which included his blood type and phone number.

"Must sell kidney. Blood group A," the ad said. "My financial situation is very difficult. I lost my job, and I need money for school for my two children."

After six months of advertising, Mr. Mircov said, his days are punctuated by hope and disappointment. He said a man from Mannheim, Germany, had offered to fly him to Germany and cover the transplant costs. But when Mr. Mircov tried to follow up, he said, the man disappeared.

A woman from Macedonia offered $24,000 for a kidney from his partner, Daniella, but that was $12,000 below her asking price. She noted that she has blood type O, which can bring a $12,000 premium on the organ market because the blood is safe for most recipients.

Mr. Mircov said he had no fear about an eventual operation or legal strictures forbidding organ sales. "It's my body, and I should be able to do what I want with it," he said.

Government officials insisted that Serbia was not so poor as to reduce people to selling their body parts, while police officials said not a single case of organ trafficking in Serbia had been prosecuted in the past 10 years. Experts who study illegal organ sales said prosecutions were rare because transplants usually took place in third countries, making them difficult to track.

Dr. Djoko Maksic, a leading nephrologist who runs the transplant program at the Military Medical Academy in Belgrade, expressed disbelief that illegal organ selling was taking place in Serbia, saying every potential donor was scrutinized and vetted by a hospital committee consisting of doctors, ethicists and lawyers.

But Milovan, 52, a former factory worker from a rural village in southern Serbia, said he "gave" his kidney to a wealthy local politician who, in return, put him on his company payroll and offered to buy him medication. The kidney was extracted at a public hospital in Belgrade, he said, with both men using forged donor cards indicating they were brothers.

Debt-ridden, Milovan, who declined to give his last name for fear of being ostracized by his neighbors, lamented that the recipient had recently cut him off, and his family said he had spent his money so quickly that he was reduced to selling eggs at a local market.

China One-Child Policy Topic

China's Cutest, Scarcest Resource*

Bloomberg Businessweek, April 2012

...Since it was put into place in 1979, China's one-child policy has had strong official backing. The National Population and Family Planning Commission, which employs about half a million people, says its efforts have averted a population surge that would have added 400 million Chinese to a population of 1.34 billion and strained the country's scarce resources. That claim is widely supported by China's top leaders, who as recently as April 10 reiterated their intention to keep birth-rates low. "The mindset for many Chinese policy makers, including a large share of the public, is still back like it was 30 to 40 years ago," says Wang Feng, senior fellow and director at the Brookings-Tsinghua Center for Public Policy at Tsinghua University in Beijing. "The belief is that the Chinese people like to have many children, and that unless the government does something extraordinary to deal with that, China will be doomed by a population explosion."

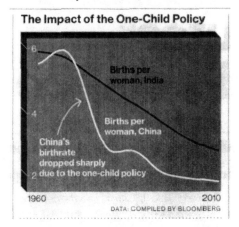

The Impact of the One-Child Policy

Births per woman, India

Births per woman, China

China's birthrate dropped sharply due to the one-child policy

1960   2010

DATA: COMPILED BY BLOOMBERG

Those attitudes date to the period just after China's Cultural Revolution ended in 1976, when the economy suffered huge shortages and food rationing was common. The demographic results of the one-child policy have been dramatic. In 1966 the average Chinese couple had about six children. Birth-rates have dropped to around 1.5 children now, which means China's population will likely peak at 1.4 billion people before 2030. Couples in the U.S. average roughly two children.

To date, China has enjoyed what economists call the "demographic dividend," with a growing labor force contributing about 0.9 percent annual economic growth, according to World Bank estimates. That dividend will disappear when the working-age population peaks at 1 billion, then starts to shrink, in 2013. While china today has some 120 million people aged 20 to 24, that's expected to drop more than 20 percent in the next decade, according to the United Nations Department of Economic and Social Affairs.

Abuses Cited in Enforcing China Policy of One Child*

The New York Times, Dec. 2010

Thirty years after it introduced some of the world's most sweeping population-control measures, the Chinese government continues to use a variety of coercive family planning tactics, from financial penalties for households that violate the restrictions to the forced sterilization of women who have already had one child, according to a report issued by a human rights group.

The report, published Tuesday by Chinese Human Rights Defenders, documents breadwinners who lose their jobs after the birth of a second child [and] campaigns that reward citizens for reporting on the reproductive secrets of their neighbors...

...Although most of the abuses documented in the report are not new, its authors are seeking to highlight the darker side of birth-control restrictions at a time when the public debate has largely focused on whether China's family-planning policy has been too successful for its own good. This year as the nation marked the 30th anniversary of the so-called one-child policy, officials have been praising such measures for preventing 400 million births. A smaller population, they argue, has helped fuel China's astounding economic growth by reducing the demands on food production, education and medical care.

* Secured from the Internet

Some demographers, however, argue that plummeting fertility rates and a rapidly aging population are reasons enough to ease the rules. Sociologists fret about the surfeit of unmarried men—the result of selective abortions that favor sons—and the demands on only children forced to care for elderly parents.

On Monday, the director of the National Population Family Planning Commission sought to put to rest any speculation about a change in the status quo, saying the current policies would remain in place through 2015.

Groups like Chinese Human Rights Defenders say the current family-planning policies should be abolished altogether. "The state's role in shaping the population should be through incentives and by encouraging couples to have fewer children through education," said Wang Songlian, a researcher who worked on the report. "They should not be using coercion and violence."

Juvenile Justice Topic

Juvenile Justice System Breeds Adult Criminals*
LiveScience, July 17, 2009.

When boys are placed in juvenile delinquency centers, they are more likely to be incarcerated as adults compared to similarly troubled kids who avoid a brush with the system early in life, a new study suggests.

Researchers say their findings suggest the system itself creates a "culture of deviance" in a house of crime contagion, where young boys learn additional bad tricks that land them back in jail later.

"For boys who had been through the *juvenile justice system*, compared to boys with similar histories without judicial involvement, the odds of adult judicial interventions increased almost seven-fold," said study co-author Richard E. Tremblay, a professor of psychology, pediatrics and psychiatry at the University of Montreal in Canada.

While the study involved only boys in Montreal, the researchers note that the juvenile justice system in the province of Quebec has a reputation of being among the best.

"The more intense the help given by the juvenile justice system, the greater was its negative impact," Tremblay said. "Most countries spend considerable financial resources to fund programs and institutions that group deviant youths together in order to help them. The problem is that delinquent behavior is contagious, especially among adolescents. Putting deviant adolescents together creates a culture of deviance, which increases the likelihood of continued criminal behavior."

Tremblay and colleagues analyzed data on 779 boys from 53 schools in poor neighborhoods. The boys were interviewed every year from age 10 to 17.

By their mid-20s, some 17.6 percent of participants ended up with adult criminal records including homicide (17.9 percent); arson (31.2 percent); prostitution (25.5 percent); drug possession (16.4 percent) and impaired driving (8.8 percent).

The results are detailed in the *Journal of Child Psychology and Psychiatry*.

Tremblay said there are two potential solutions:

"The first is to implement prevention programs before adolescence when problem children are more responsive," he said. "The second is to minimize the concentration of problem youths in juvenile justice programs, thereby reducing the risk of peer contagion." This study was funded by the Canadian Institutes of Health Research and other organizations.

Kids should never be tried as adults*
CNN OPINION February 18, 2010
Robert Schwartz, Special to CNN

About 20 years ago, 9-year-old Cameron Kocher fired a rifle out of a window of his home in upstate Pennsylvania and hit his 7-year-old neighbor, who was riding on a snowmobile, and killed her.

The prosecutor decided to try the 9-year-old as an adult. When the charge is murder, Pennsylvania is one of a handful of states that has no lower age limit for trying children as adults.

The district attorney argued that Cameron had lied when asked about the shooting -- and lying is something that adults do. The trial judge subsequently agreed to keep Cameron's case in adult court. The boy had seemed normal, the judge said, so there was nothing for the juvenile justice system to treat. Cameron had also dozed during pretrial motions, which showed "a lack of remorse."

* Secured from the Internet

Cameron stayed home on bail -- which is available to "adults" -- while his case was argued in appellate courts. He eventually pleaded guilty to a lesser charge and was placed on probation. He received no treatment and had no further involvement with the justice system.

Jump ahead 20 years, to the Western Pennsylvania prosecution of Jordan Brown, who was 11 when he was charged as an adult with shooting to death his father's pregnant fiancée. Jordan's attorneys have asked the trial judge to remand his case to juvenile court. The judge has taken the motion under advisement. It should be an easy decision.

There are common-sense reasons to keep Jordan in the juvenile system. Ask any parents of an 11-year-old if they think their child is really just a small adult!

If Jordan is adjudicated delinquent, the juvenile justice system can keep him until his 21st birthday. That is an extraordinary amount of time for an 11-year-old. It is certainly long enough to serve the needs of public protection, and enough time to rehabilitate a child. Indeed, studies routinely show that in these cases, the juvenile justice system protects the public better than the criminal justice system.

If common sense isn't enough, examine the recent science on adolescent development.

In the early part of the decade, researchers for the MacArthur Foundation Research Network on Adolescent Development and Juvenile Justice found that teenagers are less blameworthy than adults, and that their capacities change significantly over the course of adolescence.

The researchers found what many of us were trying to say years earlier about Cameron Kocher: that at the age of 9, he simply couldn't process information and plan a crime like an adult.

The MacArthur Foundation Research Network recognized that legal sanctions for misbehavior should not be based only on the harm a youth causes, but on the youth's culpability.

Most people would agree. Every day, different defendants receive different sentences even if they caused the same harm. This is because defendants differ in culpability, or blameworthiness. At no other time are these differences more pronounced than during adolescence, when youths struggle with their immaturity, undeveloped decision-making abilities, impulsiveness, lack of future orientation and susceptibility to negative peer pressure.

Recent brain imaging technology reinforces the adolescent development literature. From the prefrontal cortex to the limbic area, the teenage brain is undergoing dramatic changes during adolescence in ways that affect teens' ability to reason, to weigh consequences for their decisions and to delay gratification long enough to make careful short- and long-term choices.

In their 2008 book "Rethinking Juvenile Justice," MacArthur researchers Dr. Laurence Steinberg and Elizabeth Scott concluded that young people under age 15 should never be tried as adults.

Steinberg and Scott make clear that mitigation because of youth -- the fact that teens are less blameworthy than adults -- is not the same as an excuse. That is, trying youths in juvenile court is not the same as absolving them of responsibility.

Ten years under juvenile court supervision, for an 11-year-old, is a very long time. The point is that while youths should be punished for their crimes, it should be done in a developmentally appropriate way. Any parent would know that it makes little sense to punish a 10-year-old the same as a 17-year-old.

Another finding of the MacArthur Research Network was that young adolescents are not competent enough to be defendants. Young teens lack the skills to consult with their lawyers and shape trial strategy.

Think of Cameron Kocher, who couldn't even stay awake for his pretrial motions. Imagine Jordan Brown, now all of 12 years old, advising his lawyer on approaches to cross-examining witnesses, or discussing the pros and cons of pleading guilty.

It is in society's enlightened self-interest to keep young teens in the juvenile justice system, where public safety concerns can be addressed and young offenders can be held accountable and be rehabilitated. This is common sense. An 11-year-old is not an adult and should never be treated like one.

CPSIA information can be obtained at www.ICGtesting.com
Printed in the USA
LVOW11s0338271213

366879LV00002B/2/P

9 780988 290235